Give
Them
Poetry!

A Guide for Sharing Poetry with Children K–8

Glenna Sloan

Foreword by Douglas Florian

Teachers College, Columbia University
New York and London

Published by Teachers College Press, 1234 Amsterdam Avenue, New York, NY 10027

"Oysters" and "Sawfish" from IN THE SWIM. Copyright © 1997 by Douglas Florian, used with permission of Harcourt, Inc.

"If I Have More Candy" and "Send My Spinach" from BING, BANG, BOING. Copyright © 1994 by Douglas Florian, used with permission of Harcourt, Inc.

"Cinquain" from FOR ME TO SAY by David McCord (Little Brown, 1970). Used with permission of Little, Brown Publishers.

"Couplet" from TAKE SKY by David McCord (Little Brown, 1962). Used with permission of Little, Brown Publishers.

"Foul Shot" by Ted Hoey from READ MAGAZINE, Vol. 35, No. 9, p. 29. Used with permission of Weekly Reader Corporation.

Portions of Chapter 1 appeared first as "Poetry and Linguistic Power" by Glenna Sloan in *Teaching and Learning Literature* (TALL), September/October 1998. Vol. 8, No. 1, pp. 69–76.

In examples throughout the book, poems not otherwise credited are by the author.

Library of Congress Cataloging-in-Publication Data

Sloan, Glenna Davis, 1930–
    Give them poetry! : a guide for sharing poetry with children K–8 / Glenna Sloan ; foreword by Douglas Florian.
        p. cm. — (Language and literacy series)
    Includes bibliographical references and index.
    ISBN 0-8077-4368-2 (cloth : alk. paper) — ISBN 0-8077-4367-4 (pbk. : alk. paper)
        1. Poetry—Study and teaching (Elementary)   2. Language arts (Elementary)
    I. Title.   II. Language and literacy series (New York, N.Y.)

    LB1575.S54 2003
    372.64—dc21   2003040293

ISBN 0-8077-4367-4 (paper)
ISBN 0-8077-4368-2 (cloth)

Printed on acid-free paper

Manufactured in the United States of America

10   09   08   07   06   05   04   03   8   7   6   5   4   3   2   1

To the students in My Children's Literature Classes
Queens College, The City University of New York

Contents

Foreword

Are you afraid of poetry? Have you been attacked by a terror dactyl?
Are you spooked by spores of spondee?
Then you've come to the write place!
Does the *Iliad* make you feel ill? Does the *Odyssey* strike you as odd?
Then you've come to the write place!
Have you lost your poetic license? Have you been fined $50 for
    alliteration in front of your building?
Then you've come to the write place!
The poetry place. Where you can outdo your onomatapeers and sail
    to an Imagi-nation.
How do you teach children to read and write great poetry?
For starters, take a poem home. Cook it dinner. Feed the meter. Just
    don't use too much basal.
Sing for it.
Dance with it. It's already got rhythm.
Immerse yourself in verse.
Chant to your children.
Play with words in a wordplayground. You're allowed to!
Be verboast!
Invent new words. Reinvent new words. Your students do it every day,
    pun-knowingly.
Have elephun with an elephat elephant.
Listen to rap music. Get a rap sheet.
Resound with the sound of words. Say, "Spooooon." Look how much
    it holds in its round form. Not like the sharp "fork" Ouch!
Stringwordstogether.
Take   words   apart.
Study nature, naturally. It's eelementary.
Have a field day with your kids in a field guide. Did you know that the
Paper Birch is used to make ice cream sticks, toothpicks, and
    broomsticks. I read that in a field guide to trees.
Catch a quatrain out of town.

Rap out, tap out syllables on your desk. That's what they're built for,
You know.
Always Avoid Alliteration. Oh wait, is that alliterative?
Alliteration teaches letter-acy. As do riddles.
Use legions of illusions and allusions.
To rhyme or not to rhyme?
It's not a crime to rhyme all the time. In my prime I could rhyme on a
dime.
Then there's repetition repetition repetition.
And acrostics.
Acoustic acrostics are not for agnostics:
There was an agnostic.
He wrote an acrostic.
Envision his shame
On seeing his name.

Find lost and found poems.
And funny sound poems.
Writing haiku is easy. Just spend forty years alone in the woods and
Put it all down in 22 syllables.
Haiku master Issa is "as is" jumbled, because that is what he strove
for.
Study the famous and infamous poets. Like Lear:

There was a young person named Lear.
Penned many a limerick, dear.
His hair then turned gray,
And he passed away,
But, *funny*, the poems are still here!

Or Robert Frost:

Robert Frost was averse
To his sister's free verse.
How tersely he'd curse her,
And vice versa.

Carpet your classroom with Walt to Walt Whitman.
Cook up some Robert Frosting and serve it with hot Sara Teasdale.
Make sense out of nonsense verse.
Explore naughty taunting verse. I think we're going from bad to werse.
Chill with silly, willy-nilly.

Twist some tongues, twist some tongues, twist some tongues.
Be a multiculture vulture.
A good place to start and to stay: the Native American Shonto Begay.
Don't be picky: choose a Nikki (Giovanni or Grimes).
You can't go wrong with Janet Wong.
Get your poems in good shape. Have them run laps around the bard.

Fix them with sixty sit-ups.
      y off in a rage, kick those poems right   off
  I   the
  f   page
If they
Choose to muse on music.
Take the mystery out of history.

Poetry can *move* you
And you can move to it:
Rap or tap, or snap or clap,
You needn't even sit.

Once again, I'm at my wit's end, so I'll stop all this pun-ishment. But I'm leaving you in good hands (and feet for this *is* poetry): those of the prolific terrific Professor Glenna Sloan, a hands-on teacher of children's literature at my alma mater, Queens College. For years I've seen her motivate, captivate, elucidate, levitate, celebrate, and not to mention, educate her students. She's got the write stuff!

—Douglas Florian

Introduction

I am a ghostwriter for much of this book. A considerable amount of the material for it comes from the experiences of dozens of teachers in my graduate class, Poetry for Children, over the past 20-plus years. Our collaboration, through in-class activities and the teachers' research in their classrooms, provides persuasive evidence of the potential value of poetry and verse in literacy development. Based on an actual poetry class for adults, the book can serve as a program of study for teachers, librarians, parents, or anyone else interested in "giving children poetry."

"Poetry," declares literary theorist Northrop Frye (1963b), "the main body of which is verse, is always the central powerhouse of a literary education" (p. 25). There being relatively little research on how poetry and verse might affect literacy development, we don't have much hard evidence to support his claim. I believe that the reason for the dearth of empirical data is clear. Few educators are interested in studying poetry's effect on learning to read and write, for a couple of probable reasons. Many know little about poetry beyond what they learned in high school, knowledge that often results in the mistaken belief that poetry is an esoteric genre, full of mysterious metaphors that only certain elite minds can fathom. Some simply don't take it seriously, believing that in comparison to prose, it strains to communicate through artifice and artiness. In any case, these are the beliefs of many of the teachers who enroll in my class on children's poetry.

In my experience, teachers are unusually conscientious. Over the years some come to the poetry class as poetry lovers, but more often my students are those who fear and dislike poetry because of unfortunate experiences with its study in high school and college English literature classes. As a result, these teachers avoid poetry reading and writing in their classrooms. This leads them to worry that limiting their students' poetic experience shortchanges them, a concern that makes the teachers willing to risk joining a college class to learn something about poetry and how to bring it to their children. One objective of the class is to dispel the mystique that surrounds poetry for many people, "to take it down from its pedestal," in the words of children's poet and teacher *extraordinaire*, Eve Merriam (Sloan, 1981).

In the class, both lovers and nonlovers of poetry learn, among other lessons, those Eve taught in her workshops: Poetry can be game-like, puzzle-like both in its form and in the sport and playfulness of its language. In poetry there is something for every interest, every ability. Poetic devices, musical effects like rhythmic repetition and alliteration, metaphor and simile, all have natural appeal because they are in fact extensions of children's own speech and thought processes. Further, poetry, which ranges from simple jingles to rhythmic complexities, is meant to be experienced *out loud.*

Give Them Poetry!, the words of the book's title, were spoken often by Leland B. Jacobs, for years professor of children's literature at Teachers College, Columbia University, and himself a children's poet. I was a classroom teacher in elementary and middle school for 16 years before I became his student, and my teaching experience had convinced me that literacy begins in hearts, not heads; Dr. Jacobs, a professor who regularly worked in elementary classrooms to promote literacy, confirmed this conviction. Children who never feel delight and amazement at the wonderful things words can be made to do are unlikely to be keen about making the considerable effort it takes to read and write them.

In literature, poetry especially, language is ideally at its best: rhythmic, evocative, playful, witty. "Give them poetry!" Professor Jacobs thundered to his classes at Teachers College. "Poetry will make children take an interest in words. Without that interest, they'll never care much about reading and writing." Just how to give children poetry so they are turned on rather than turned off by it, is the subject of much of this book in words often echoing those heard in Leland Jacobs's lectures.

Give Them Poetry! is organized in five chapters. Chapter 1, "Poetry and Literacy," makes a case for poetry's role in the development of literacy. Chapter 2, "The Poetry Class," discusses questions teachers raise in my college poetry class, among them: To teach poetry well, what do you have to know about poetry? In bringing children and poetry together, what strategies work best? Answers to these questions are supplied in part by the educators themselves from their own classroom experiences. Chapter 3, "Writer's Workshop," deals with writing poetry, the flip side of poetry reading and study. In Chapter 4, "Poetry Applied," examples are presented of classroom projects in elementary and middle school in which poetry is used to stimulate interest in language and motivate efforts in reading and writing. Chapter 5 contains "Words of Wisdom" from both children and teachers. Some students in the poetry class are not classroom teachers; these often choose, working with their own or borrowed children, to undertake projects similar to those conducted in classrooms. To encourage parents and other care givers to share poetry with children, the chapter includes accounts of poetry projects undertaken *outside* of classrooms. The chapter concludes with a selection of insightful comments from teachers in the poetry class concerning what they learned about giving children poetry. The last words are from the children.

Throughout the book are quotations by master teacher/poets and resources that teachers find useful: lists of noted children's poets and titles of notable reference material on teaching poetry.

CHAPTER 1

Poetry and Literacy

Most of us do manage to learn to read and write, if even at a rudimentary level. But the ability to read traffic signs and sign one's name is but the beginning of literacy, which is after all a development over a lifetime. To initiate this development requires at the very least an interest in written words. Sustaining the process, moving toward true literacy, demands more. The truly literate read and write all their lives independently, responsively, and because they want to. They have moved beyond interest in words to fascination with them. Written language has cast its spell.

MAKING THE MAGIC HAPPEN

Learning to read does carry with it an element of magic. In the Introduction to *The Acts of King Arthur and His Noble Knights*, John Steinbeck (1976) writes of that magical moment when, for him, the marks on the page became words:

> I remember that words—written or printed—were devils, and books, because they gave me pain, were my enemies. Then one day, an aunt gave me a book [It was a cut version of Mallory 's *Morte D'Arthur*]. . . . I stared at the black print with hatred, and then, gradually the pages opened and let me in. The magic happened. (p. xi)

Despite all the millions of words declaimed and written by "reading experts," self-styled or otherwise, despite all the thousands of dissertation research studies devoted to the subject, the truth is that we are not at all certain how the magic happens and certainly not in complete agreement, either, about how to *make* it happen. Expert advice on the best way to make the magic of reading happen was reported in the *New York Times* on March 19, 1998. A distinguished panel, convened by the National Research Council, reviewed the reams of research on reading. Their advice was predictable and political. They advocated sounding out words (phonics); they invoked the worthy but ill-defined concept of "whole language," in this case the aspect of that philosophy that insists on using actual texts, factual and fictional, with beginning readers. There was no mention of poetry as reading material.

This is not surprising. Raised on prose or what passes for it, pragmatic Americans seem to prefer language in its utilitarian mode: as communication, as the language that gets business taken care of. Most people are likely to consider poetry to be a perverse way—albeit often a witty and ingenious one—of distorting prose statements. (This would explain our deplorable custom of ransacking a poem to uncover its *true* meaning; in other words, its *prose* translation.)

Literary theorist Northrop Frye (1970) asks us to entertain this idea.

> The greatest fallacy in the present conception of literary education is the notion that prose is the normal language of ordinary speech, and should form the center and staple of literary teaching. . . . The root of the fallacy is the assumption that prose represents the only valid form of thought, and that poetry, considered as thought, is essentially decorated or distorted prose. . . . The main principles of a coherently organized curriculum are simple enough. . . . Poetry should be at the center of all literary training, and literary prose forms the periphery. (p. 94)

In most classrooms, just the opposite is true: Poetry is at the periphery of the curriculum, if it is in sight at all. It plays only a marginal role in most classroom life, occasionally used as reading material or as a read-aloud by the teacher, but not deployed on a regular basis or in a systematic way.

But Frye (1963) persists in offering food for thought. In another place he says:

> Ideally, our literary education should begin, not with prose, but with such things as "this little pig went to market"—with verse rhythms reinforced by physical assault. The infant who gets bounced on somebody's knee to the rhythm of "Ride a cock horse" does not need a footnote telling him that Banbury Cross is twenty miles northeast of Oxford. All he needs is to get bounced. If he is, he is beginning to develop a response to poetry in the place where it ought to start. For verse is closely related to dance and song; it is also closely related to the child 's own speech, which is full of chanting and singing, as well as primitive verse forms like the war-cry and the taunt-song. At school the study of verse is supplemented by the study of prose, and a good prose style in both speech and writing is supposed to be aimed at. But poetry, the main body of which is verse, is always the central powerhouse of a literary education. (pp. 24–26)

Now, how can he be so sure that this is true? There is relatively little research on how poetry and verse might affect literacy development. If

> "A poem makes you aware of language so that even in prose you can enjoy using words more because you know what tricks they can do and what they cannot do" (Eve Merriam, 1962, p. 3).

poetry generally is relegated to the position of an unnecessary frill on the edge of the curriculum, how can Northrop Frye insist so emphatically on its power to develop literacy?

THE PROMISE OF POETRY

Although they are not controlled studies in the scientific way or even ethnographic descriptions in the social scientific way, there *are* proofs of the power of poetry in a literary education. Dylan Thomas's father, a grammar school teacher, read to his son Shakespeare and only Shakespeare from the time he was a toddler. Those familiar with the sonorous cadences of Thomas's poetry are not surprised to hear this. William Butler Yeats, considered by many the greatest poet of the twentieth century, when he was 8 or 9 listened as his father read aloud rhythmic romances like "The Lay of the Last Minstrel." Brendan Gill, for decades a writer of distinguished prose for *The New Yorker*, was paid a dollar a line by his father to memorize verse. Even a sonnet net good pay in the 1920s. But the payoff was even greater in the smooth, seemingly effortless style that undoubtedly came to Gill from the store of poetic cadences he held in his head.

The prolific poet and playwright, Eve Merriam, grew up near Philadelphia. As a child, she attended many D'Oyly Carte productions of Gilbert and Sullivan works. Those who enjoy the polysyllabic playfulness of the rhymes in Gilbert and Sullivan operas will hear their echoes in Eve Merriam's poetry. She was also influenced by the tumbling word clusters of Gerard Manley Hopkins and the originality of imagery she found in W. H. Auden's work. She says, "There is a line of his that I can never forget every day of my life and I can't even remember what poem it's in. But he talks about himself as 'a fathom of earth alive in air.' And it just seemed such a wonderful image to me" (Sloan, 1981, p. 962).

Myra Cohn Livingston, another children's poet who left a rich legacy of her writing, speaks of inspiration from childhood reading. She mentions hearing Christina Rossetti's poems, in particular one in a small book bound in green that asked the question, "Who has seen the wind?" The poetry of

"There is no rhyme for silver, but a poem can do just about anything else you want it to. It can be solemn or bouncy, gay or sad—as you yourself change your own moods. A poem, in fact, is very much like you, and that is quite natural, since there is a rhythm in your own body: in your pulse, in your heart beat, in the way you breathe, laugh, or cry; in the very way you speak" (Eve Merriam, 1962, p. 1).

her childhood enchanted her, held her in thrall; the love of words it engendered compelled her to write poetry herself (Children's Book Council, 1997, pp. 31–33).

If we are what we eat, surely our language is what we read and hear. Northrop Frye (1963a), arguably the greatest literary theorist of the past century, has more to say on the subject: "What poetry can give the student is, first of all, the sense of physical movement. Poetry is not irregular lines in a book, but something very close to dance and song, something to walk down the street keeping time to" (pp. 51–52). Frye believed that experiencing the rhythms of verse, which reflect the child's own bodily rhythms, in a sense teaches the child the basics of using language. He considered it significant that the first selections "read" by a child—long before he or she goes to school—are likely to be the jingles of television commercials. He wondered why—in elementary school—we don't capitalize on this and use these familiar jingles as early reading material. When we are steeped in rhythmic language like that of nursery rhymes, language reflecting our bodily rhythms, he believed that we are more likely "to develop a speaking and prose style that comes out of the depths of personality and is a genuine expression of it" (Frye, 1963b, p.26).

Russian poet Kornei Chukovsky, in the classic, *From Two to Five* (1968), agreed. He firmly placed poetry front and center in literacy development: "Under the influence of beautiful word sequences, shaped by a pliable musical rhythm and richly melodic rhymes, the child playfully, without the least effort, strengthens his vocabulary and his sense of the structure of his native language" (p. 87). "As I educated my own children," he continued, "I tried to instill in them, from an early age, a sense of literary discrimination, of aesthetic sensibility, and thus to arm them forever against every variety of literary banality. The material that seemed to me best suited for reaching this goal was . . . the heroic epic. I read epic poetry to my children and their numerous friends" (p. 74).

> "You may not 'get' all of a poem the first time you read it, because the words and the built-in music are so concentrated. Don't let it worry you; just go on to the end and then go back and read it again" (Eve Merriam, 1962, p. 4).

THE POWER OF WORDS

I have my own proof of the power of such poetry in literacy development. The proof comes from work with an eighth grade in a suburban Toronto junior high school, where I was chair of the English Department with some say about experimentation with curriculum.

For weeks—months, actually—we immersed ourselves in Richmond Lattimore's (1951) translation of the *Iliad*. I cut some of the lengthier catalogues of names of ships and the like, but for the most part we used an unabridged text. We read this timeless tale, responding to it by talking, by writing, with artwork. But mostly we read and reread the text aloud.

Volunteers prepared favorite bits for reading aloud. We also prepared and performed narration and speeches as readers' theater scripts, hearing the effect of different voices, supplying narration, and interpreting the various characters. Slowly, the language became part of us. Through familiarity with the text, the students began to notice its special qualities and conventions. They relished the long similes.

> Hektor
> would not stay back among the mass of close-armoured Trojans,
> but as a flashing eagle makes his plunge upon other
> flying birds as these feed in a swarm by the river,
> so Hektor steered the course of his outrush straight for a vessel
> with dark prows. (Lattimore, 1951, p. 327)

They reveled in the rich language of description and action:

> glorious Hektor held out his arms to his baby,
> who shrank back to his fair-girdled nurse's bosom
> screaming, and frightened at the aspect of his own father,
> terrified as he saw the bronze and the crest with its horse-hair,
> nodding dreadfully, as he thought, from the peak of the helmet.
> Then his beloved father laughed out, and his honored mother,
> and at once glorious Hektor lifted from his head the helmet

> "It's particularly important to do a lot of reading if you think you might want to write some poems yourself" (Paul Janeczko in Copeland, 1992, p. 54).

and laid it in all its shining upon the ground.
Then taking up his dear son he tossed him about in his arms,
and kissed him. (Lattimore, 1951, p. 165)

The *Iliad* was for many weeks the center and sole focus of our entire English language arts program. No parent or administrator objected to this radical curriculum when they read what the children were writing. And we were never bored. Try in-depth study of something worthwhile; it is far more satisfying than dozens of brief encounters.

Earlier in the term we had studied Greek mythology. In fact, our study of the *Iliad* grew out of the students' interest in these tales. When the students decided that it was time to try composing an original poem in the epic style, the myths were often the subject of choice. Heather Mackey chose to tell the story of Arachne. Here is an excerpt:

Hearken, ye gods, to the tale of the immortal Athene,
who decreed the fate of the boastful Arachne,
she who evermore shall stand as a warning to mortals
who dare defy the gods. For now,
she weaves unceasingly
every day and all night.
In the land of the Achaians dwelt a maiden,
fair Arachne of the prattling tongue.
Always, she must tell of her skill at the loom.
So proud was she that her fame spread
to all the ends of the earth.
"Even Athene is not my equal," spoke vain Arachne.
And so the tale spread.
Hearing it, the gods' messenger, Mercury,
he of the winged feet, hastened to Athene
and told her of Arachne's boast.
Pallas Athene, angered, spoke:
"I go now unto Lydia, the land
of the green meadows,
to warn this proud maiden,

> "For me, the finest poems are those that use metaphor well, because they enable us to see, for the first time, images we might never have imagined for ourselves" (Myra Cohn Livingston, 1991, p. 94).

Arachne of the swift fingers,
of her fate."
So she spoke, and sent her sacred owl
winging in swift flight earthward
on stealthy pinions,
silent as soft-stepping Hecate
covers the earth at the end of the day
with her veil of darkness. . . .

Another student, Laurence Woodruff, who had read all of Rosemary Sutcliff's historical novels, wrote a 75-line poem in three "books." For me, the effort clearly illustrates how the rhythms and devices of the *Iliad* were absorbed by the poet in this poem about Marius, a young galley slave.

As he entered the hold, they sprang upon him,
As lions spring upon the unwary buck,
And they grappled with him and bound him.
When morning dawned, the boy awoke
To feel sharp pain in his head
Where they had struck him with a wooden club;
Where bonds had been, there was now a shackle,
And he was chained to a bench with others, unlucky,
A slave in the galleys of
King Solomon's Navy.
As the days became weeks,
And the weeks months,
He learned the ways of the rowers
From the man, Jason, who was his friend.
So also he learned to eat the black bread;
And, as jackals fight for the scraps
On the bony carcass that is left to them
By the lions, so he fought
For the scraps flung to them by his master.
But, above all, he learned to hate. . . .

The great epic echoes in these poems, just two examples chosen from a full class's compositions. Although I couldn't follow these students to find out, I feel confident that our intensive study of the *Iliad* carried over into their speaking and writing, bringing to their literacy development, even if in small measure, a "sense of wit and heightened intelligence, resulting from seeing disciplined words marching along in metrical patterns and in their inevitably right order, . . . [the poem's] rhythm and leisure slowly soaking into the body and its wit and concreteness into the mind" (Frye, 1963b, pp. 25–26).

Frye's own fluent, rhythmical prose style is a testimony to the potential power of the words in great literature. It results from a lifetime of hearing and reading finely wrought language, which began when his mother read aloud to him, mostly from the Bible, but also from Dickens and Charles Kingsley (Ayre, 1989).

SOUND LANGUAGE

In the 1960s and early 1970s, author and educator Bill Martin developed a series of basal readers like no others published before or since. His *Sounds of Language* series for elementary and middle school, published by Holt, was before its time in featuring genuine literature to develop literacy. What was more unusual, he used poetry and verse *as reading material.* The first primer, *Sounds I Remember* (Martin, 1970), includes fail-safe items chosen for their rhythmic repetitiveness and their familiarity to beginning readers: "Happy birthday to you"; "The ABC song"; "One, two, buckle my shoe"; that perennial favorite: "The wheels of the bus/Go round and round"; "Little Peter Rabbit had a flea upon his ear," and more.

Martin agreed with Northrop Frye that the rhymes and jingles, the familiar verse children *already knew*, would make the best reading material for beginners. Frye (1970) wonders why elementary educators fail to capitalize on the young child's propensity for and delight in riddles, conundrums, tongue twisters, rhymes, and puns. Surely their oral lore, full of chanting and singing, is the perfect first reading material for them. As Frye points out, young children's repetitious chanting of polysyllabic words that catch their fancy makes it clear "that the child understands [instinctively] what many adults do not, that verse is a more direct and primitive way of conventionalizing speech than prose is" (p. 96). Chukovsky (1968) concurs: "In the beginning of our childhood we are all 'versifiers;' it is only later that we learn to speak in prose" (p. 64).

Bill Martin's fine readers were never given a fair chance in the classroom. They were tucked away on a shelf for occasional use. I believe this

"Perhaps you'll read a poem out loud by yourself, or a group may want to chant in unison. Maybe you'll make up some dances, or mime gestures, or put together some mini-dramas around a particular poem. Whatever you do, please do it unquietly Out Loud" (Eve Merriam, 1973, p. 4).

was because they were so full of beauty and pleasurable material, just the opposite of the Dick and Jane-style basal readers. There will always be those who believe that learning to read, any learning, to be effective, must involve hard and distasteful work. (The Dick and Jane days were the time when the clunky prose of bad basal readers was preferred over fine stories and poetry as reading material.) Deathly prose like this in a 1976 reader usurped the place of fine writing in children's literary upbringing:

Al has a tan cat, Kit.
Kit, the tan cat, can sit
Kit, the tan cat, can nap
Kit sat and had a nap
A fat cat ran to Kit.
Kit ran to a pit. Kit sat at the pit.
The fat cat ran to the pit.
(Rasmussen & Goldberg, 1976, pp. 6–7)

Later, in ostensibly more enlightened times, textbook publishers began including in readers selections from actual published literary works for children. Misguided, they set about simplifying—basalizing—literary language until its magic became merely mundane. It's as though children, those players with language, lovers of language, can't recognize and read words at their best.

CHAPTER 2

The Poetry Class

Queens College is one of few graduate schools to offer a master's degree with a specialization in children's literature. Since the early 1980s, the program has flourished, its courses, covering a wide range of subjects in children's literature, always fully enrolled. Poetry for Children is no exception. During the first session, in the interest of collaboratively setting goals and objectives for the class, I often ask students, most of them teachers pursuing a master's degree, why they enrolled in this elective course. Here, verbatim, are typical responses:

"I want to help my children write poetry, but I don't know the best way to get started." "I hated studying poetry in high school so I avoid it with my kids, and that's not good for them." "I write what I think is poetry, but I really don't know what poetry *is*." "I know there are good children's poets out there—one came to my school and he was great—I want to find out about more." "I've always loved reading and writing poetry, but I don't know much about poetry written especially for children and I want to learn about it." "My first graders love poetry right now and I want to keep it that way; as I got into higher grades myself, I began to hate poetry study."

Together we build the curriculum for the weekly sessions ahead, striving to practice in the college class what we preach for the elementary and middle school classroom. Among the objectives for the course are:

- to become familiar with a variety of poetry and verse suitable for children;
- to study through inquiry and discovery technical aspects of the genre;
- to consider the importance of poetry and verse to linguistic and imaginative development;
- to practice ways of presenting poetry to children and engaging them in presentation;
- to explore ways to make poetry a central part of classroom life;
- to develop skill in evaluating and selecting poetry for use with specific groups of children;

> "Poetry is as simple as dirt. It's ice cream and cake. . . . I believe
> that when we clear away the mist and myth that encode poetry,
> we will discover a delightful and universally popular art form" (Brod
> Bagert in Copeland, 1993, p. 54)

- to learn ways of encouraging and helping children to write poetry
  and verse.

A description of what we do in the college class follows. All the objectives stated above are important for our consideration, but we place particular emphasis on learning about children's poets and the poetry they write. Space does not permit a full or direct discussion of every course objective listed, but the suggested readings and accounts of teachers' classroom experiences will help the reader fill in the blanks. For example, helpful books on incorporating poetry across the curriculum (which will be discussed in Chapter 4) include *Three Voices: An Invitation to Poetry Across the Curriculum* (Cullinan, Scala, & Schroder, 1995) and *Using Poetry Across the Curriculum* (Chatton, 1995).

Learn by doing is the philosophy that guides the course. First, if teachers wish to give children poetry with confidence, it is essential that the teachers become personally familiar with a wide variety of children's poetry. Next, to ensure that learners internalize knowledge through discovery, teachers need to puzzle out for themselves as many facts as possible about how poetry works, as teachers and learners talk together about poems and try to write them. Then, it is necessary for the grown-up students to apply their knowledge in their elementary and middle school classrooms, with the needs and interests of specific students in mind.

GETTING TO KNOW CHILDREN'S POETS
AND THEIR POETRY

One of our first learning experiences involves consulting an expert source on children's poetry. We view a sound filmstrip, *Poetry Explained* (1980), by outstanding children's poet Karla Kuskin. The filmstrip, meant primarily for elementary and middle school children, is filled with insights to benefit those of any age. For too many, poetry is buried in mystique; Karla brushes aside mystery.

Poems can rhyme or not, she tells us, although rhyme, if it is not forced or clichéd, is satisfying to young ears. Poems may be on any subject under the sun and on many that are not, for although ideas for poems can come from memories and feelings, they also can come from the imagination.

A poem can be as few as two words: "Bug/Ugh!" Kuskin illustrates, using a jump rope rhyme of nonsense words, the importance of rhythm to poetry. She shows how poems often are built of images and repetitious patterns. She emphasizes the importance of strong, vivid images that appeal to all our senses, (although not necessarily all at once). By presenting in the filmstrip a poem in prose form, she emphasizes that the very arrangement of words on the page is an important aspect of poetry. This accomplished poet makes us feel that poetry is accessible, that it belongs to everyone. Her warm invitation into the world of poetry is what the teachers and other adults in the class need in order to feel welcome and at home in a new place.

Leafing Through Anthologies

Getting to know children's poets and their poetry comes first for the college students. This is knowledge they eventually will share with the children in their classes back in elementary and middle school.

Immersion is the key word. Armed with lists of noted poets and outstanding anthologies, we begin reading, reading, reading, and sharing in the college class. While lists of poets serve as guides, we are mindful of Eve Merriam's words: "I prefer browsing to heading directly with a certified list in hand. Serendipity is the best . . . the lovely leafing through anthologies" (Children's Book Council, 1997, p. 63).

An array of anthologies is brought to the college class by instructor and students, just as similar volumes soon will appear in the classrooms where the teachers/college students teach. In small groups, my students, after prior practice in private to ensure the most effective presentation, read aloud their favorites to each other. They note how anthologies of poetry for children are organized because they are required, during the term, to create anthologies of their own.

An anthology is a collection of poems, but bear in mind that there are different types of anthologies. A general anthology like *Reflections on a Gift of Watermelon Pickle* (Dunning, Lueders, & Smith, 1967) has poems by many poets on a variety of subjects. A specialized anthology has poems on one subject by several poets. Two examples are: *Food Fight: Poets Join the Fight Against Hunger with Poems to Favorite Foods* (Rosen, 1996) and a collection by Nancy Willard entitled *Step Lightly: Poems for the Journey* (1998). In an individual anthology there are poems by a single poet; they may be on one subject or many. *Advice for a Frog* (Schertle, 1995) uses a variety of forms to

"In looking for poems and poets, don't dwell on the boundaries of style, or time, or even of countries and cultures. Think of yourself rather as a member of a single, recognizable tribe. Expect to understand poems of other eras and cultures. Expect to feel intimate with the distant voice" (Mary Oliver, 1994, p. 11).

create 14 portraits in words of endangered or extinct species. Animals are also the subject of Barbara Esbensen's inspired poems in *Words with Wrinkled Knees* (1986).

Ever on the watch for material to enrich every subject they teach, the teachers look for poems on science and social studies topics, mathematics, music, language itself. The New York State Standards for Language Arts require that students read and write in a variety of genres, including poetry. Discovering, through their reading, the wealth of poems available on math, social studies, and other curriculum areas, teachers, surprised and pleased, vow to incorporate poems into all the work of the classroom. That includes using them to introduce units, to illustrate that topics may be understood through use of multiple genres, and as reading material related to curriculum topics.

A word of caution in the matter of "using" poetry in the service of other areas of study: Poetry should be allowed to develop literacy on its own most of the time; in large enough quantities and in pleasurable circumstances, poetry has the power to motivate readers and inspire writers. In incorporating poetry into the curriculum, the key word to remember is *enrichment*.

General Anthologies. As they browse in collections of children's poetry, the students in my college class examine them critically.

- Overall, is the book attractive and inviting?
- Are the topics those that are likely to interest children?
- Is a variety of poetic forms represented?
- Is there a balance of old and new poetry and verse?
- What poems are representative of timeless appeal?

Fig 2.1 is a list of general anthologies proven to be excellent sources of children's poetry.

Personal Anthologies. The teacher's personal anthology is an invaluable teaching resource. Here is a place to save favorites and store key poems related to curriculum topics. Here, appropriate poems are nearby when it

> "Poems can be used anywhere. This is part of the whole-language philosophy, where you cross-fertilize ideas. Poetry is both subtle and simple; often it can get difficult concepts across very effectively." (Mary Ann Hoberman in Copeland, 1993/1994, p. 58)

is time to celebrate important events in children's lives. Poems need to become a regular, familiar part of daily classroom ritual rather than an occasional read-aloud. There are poems, for instance, about sibling relationships and the birth of new brothers and sisters, about the acquiring of new shoes, about learning to whistle, about the loss of a first tooth, about trips to the zoo.

Invariably, the teachers in the poetry class tell me that one of their children's favorite classroom books is the teacher's own collection of poems. This is true partly because the personal volume contains familiar good things to read, but mostly it is because their teacher created it.

I visited the kindergarten classroom of a teacher who had been a student in the poetry class years before. Her fat photograph album crammed with poems stood in a prominent place in the library corner, its once-white cover smudged, the pages well worn from good use.

The teachers/students discover that common to most anthologies are sections such as weather, friends, family, animals, humor, city life. They note that usually a variety of poetic forms is included: riddles, story poems, haiku. The teachers' selections will reflect their own interests, as well as the needs, interests, age, and ability of their students. As they collect poems for their own anthologies, to be mounted in full-page photo albums, (perhaps decorated with drawings or cutouts from magazines) the teachers exercise their own creativity in choice of poems and arrangement of selections. The possibilities for topics and organization are endless. Teachers include sections on poems they loved as children, poems they have written themselves, playground rhymes and jingles, shape poems, experimental poems, favorite songs. The sky's the limit. For unpublished personal anthologies, there are no costs to pay or copyright permissions to secure. One essential requirement must always be met: The author's name appears with each poem.

Back in the teachers' classrooms, as the children's interest in poetry grows and their knowledge about poetry increases, creating their own classroom anthologies becomes a priority. Teachers report high interest among their students in researching poems for this collaborative effort, and enthusiastic lobbying for the inclusion of favorites.

Figure 2.1. Outstanding Anthologies: A Selective List

Book poems: Poems from national children's book week, 1959–1998 .(1998). New York: *The* Children's Book Council.

Cole, W. (1981). *Poem stew.* New York: HarperCollins.

de Regniers, B. S. et al. (1988). *Sing a song of popcorn: every child's book of poems.* New York: Scholastic.

Koch, K., & Farrell, K. (1998). *Talking to the sun.* New York: Simon and Schuster.

In daddy's arms I am tall: African Americans celebrating fathers. (1997). New York: Lee and Low,

Mora, P. (Ed.). (2001). *Love to mama: A tribute to mothers.* New York: Lee and Low.

Nye, N. S. (1998). *The space between our footsteps: Poems and paintings from the Middle East. New York: Simon and Schuster.*

Opie, P., & Opie, I. (1992). *I saw Esau: The schoolchild's pocket book* (Illustrated by Maurice Sendak). Cambridge, MA: Candlewick.

Opie, P., & Opie, I. (1994). *The Oxford book of children's verse.* New York: Oxford University Press.

Prelutsky, J. (1983). *The random house book of poetry.* New York: Random House.

Prelutsky, J. (1986). *Read-aloud rhymes for the very young.* New York: Knopf.

Prelutsky, J. (1999). *The 20th century children's poetry treasury.* New York: Knopf.

Sutherland, Z. (1976). *The Arbuthnot anthology of children's literature, part 1: Time for poetry* (Fourth ed.). Chicago: Scott Foresman.

Collecting Poems of Different Kinds

To this point, the college class has been introduced to the study of poetry through the perusal of anthologies of all kinds. To take a closer look at children's poets and their poetry, let's look at different ways to approach this vast topic with preservice and inservice teachers.

Rich Sounds from the Past. The first of these approaches is titled Rich Sounds from the Past. Students are encouraged to find poems to share in class from the works of such poets as: Dorothy Aldis, Hilaire Belloc, the Benéts, William Blake, Robert Burns, Lewis Carroll, John Ciardi, Walter de la Mare, Emily Dickinson, T. S. Eliot, Eleanor Farjeon Rachel Field, Robert Frost, Leland B. Jacobs, Randall Jarrell, Edward Lear, Vachel Lindsay, A. A. Milne, James Reeves, Laura Richards, James Whitcomb Riley, Elizabeth Madox Roberts, Christina Rossetti, Robert Louis Stevenson, Sara Teasdale, J. R. R. Tolkien, and Walt Whitman. Since no such roster is ever complete, students are invited to add to it.

As they read, the students try to identify the characteristics of poems of the past that make them timeless favorites of children lucky enough to be introduced to them. Bright with imagery, the lilting lyrics of Christina Rossetti and Sara Teasdale easily span the decades. Edward Lear's limericks and other nonsense verse, a century and more old, tickle contemporary funny bones. The poems about famous Americans by Stephen and Rosemary Benét are as fresh as today's news. Alive forever, *The Bat-Poet* passes along Randall Jarrell's (1964) wisdom to new readers. Today's child laughs at Hilaire Belloc's macabre cautionary tales in verse that originated in Victorian times. In his poems, A. A. Milne unerringly captures the voice and viewpoint of the young child in any age.

Traditional Rhymes and Jingles. Another approach explores the oral lore that is the ancestor of children's poetry. Just as the children in their classrooms will do, the grown-up students read and collect, to share in class, examples of Mother Goose, jump-rope rhymes, taunt songs, riddles, and tongue twisters. Required reading for this segment is the classic by Iona and Peter Opie *The Language and Lore of Schoolchildren* (1959), as well as their *I Saw Esau* (1992) and *The Oxford Nursery Rhyme Book* (1955).

In their remarkable book about children's oral lore, Peter and Iona Opie (1959) quote Dylan Thomas, who observed that children "tumble and rhyme" out the school door (p. 18). They come chanting: *Oh my finger, oh my thumb, oh my belly, oh my bum,* or a similar nonsensical rhyme. They taunt: *Tell tale tit, Your tongue shall be slit.* They jump rope to rhythmic rhymes. They talk silly.

Red, white, and blue
My mother is a Jew;
My father is a Scotsman,
And I'm a kangaroo.

They delight in silly riddles, conundrums, and nonsensical inquiries that pun and play with words: *When is a sailor not a sailor? When he's a board. Can the orange box? No, but the tomato can.* They use rhyme to help them remember: *Thirty days hath September, April, June, and November,* and so on.

As Northrop Frye (1970) puts it: "The speech of a small child is full of chanting and singing, and it is clear that the child understands what many adults do not, that verse is a more direct and primitive way of convention-alizing speech than prose is" (p. 96).

Less than Literary. Poetry and verse represent a continuum, all the way from rhymes on greeting cards to Shakespeare's majestic blank verse. Folk songs, pop songs, raps, and advertising jingles from radio and TV, all appear along this continuum. The teachers in the poetry class are reminded that children delight in slogans, macabre and disgusting rhymes, nonsense verses, tongue twisters, knock-knock jokes. *Trick or treat, Smell my feet. See you later, alligator. In a while, crocodile.* They collect examples of these favorites of the young, often with the help of their own students.

According to the venerable educational adage, we must begin where children are. While adults may have forgotten childhood delight in linguistic grossness, they deny it at their peril, forgetting that good taste in poetry or anything else is developed only through experiencing both awful and ex-cellent. The wise teacher, eager to introduce children to fine poetry, if he or she is skilled in public relations, begins with what they know and like. In the college class, we discuss the fact that less than literary verse may be the key that opens the door to poetry for many children.

Many Cultures—Many Voices. Through poetry, the college students cele-brate their own and others' heritage. In this they are guided by their fellow students, beginning with poetry that represents the richly varied ethnicity of a Queens College class. Some bring poems in their family's first language to share aloud in that language. Others read aloud the powerful poems found in *I Am the Darker Brother* (Adoff, 1968) and other Adoff anthologies of African American poetry: *All the Colors of the Race* (1982), *Black Is Brown Is Tan* 1973), and *My Black Me: A Beginning Book of Black Poetry* (1974/1994).

Some researchers are sure to find the work of native Americans in col-lections compiled by Joseph Bruchac (1995, 1996a, 1996b), Shonto Begay (1995), and others; of African American writers such as Gwendolyn Brooks, Ashley Bryan, Lucille Clifton, Countee Cullen, Nikki Giovanni, Nikki Grimes, Eloise Greenfield, Langston Hughes, Angela Johnson, Angela Shelf Medearis, Walter Dean Myers, and Joyce Carol Thomas; of Latino poets Alma Flor Ada, Juan Herrera, Pat Mora, and Pablo Neruda; of advocate for Middle Eastern and international poetry, Naomi Shihab Nye; of Mexican American Gary Soto; of Korean/Chinese American Janet Wong; and of Caribbean poets John Agard and Grace Nichols.

"I became a writer because words gave me so much pleasure that I
have always wanted to sink my hands and heart into them, to see
what I can create, what will rise up, what will appear on the page"
(Pat Mora, 2000, pp. 1–2).

Back in their classrooms, many teachers invite upper elementary and
middle school children to translate simple rhymes in English into their
second language, emphasizing the imagery, because rhymes may not
translate. Poems in languages other than English appear in the teachers'
anthologies and in those compiled by their students. We conclude that
while reading aloud is essential in experiencing *any* poetry, it is crucial
to appreciation of poems in second languages.

Award-Winning Voices. Established to recognize excellence in the body of
work of a living American poet writing for children, The National Council of
Teachers of English (NCTE) Award for Excellence in Poetry For Children is
presented every 3 years. The college students examine the works of the
winners: David McCord, Aileen Fisher, Karla Kuskin, Myra Cohn Livingston,
Lilian Moore, Arnold Adoff, Eve Merriam, John Ciardi, Valerie Worth,
Barbara Esbensen, Eloise Greenfield, X. J. Kennedy, and Mary Ann Hoberman.

The NCTE journal, *Language Arts*, features profiles of these poets, usually in the final issue of the year in which the poet won the award.

Besides the NCTE poetry award winners, there are dozens of fine contemporary poets to sample, with new ones coming along each year to join
them. The International Reading Association sponsors the Lee Bennett
Hopkins Award for a Promising New Poet. Winners since the award was
initiated are: Deborah Chandra, 1995; Kristine O'Connell George, 1998;
Craig Crist-Evans, 2001.

Students read and bring in to share examples of works by contempo-
rary poets like the NCTE poetry award winners and other fine poets
who have distinguished themselves writing for children, among them: Byrd
Baylor, Harry Behn, Brod Bagert, N. M. Bodecker, Charles Causley, Deborah
Chandra, Joanna Cole, Kali Dakos, Rebecca Dotlich, Paul Fleischman, Joan
Bransfield Graham, Avis Harley, David Harrison, Mary Ann Hoberman, Ted
Hughes, Dennis Lee, J. Patrick Lewis, Colin McNaughton, Jack Prelutsky,
Michael Rosen, Alice Schertle, Shel Silverstein, Judith Viorst, Nancy Willard,
Jane Yolen, and Charlotte Zolotow.

It is a challenge to stay current with the many poets newly published
each year. One source of reviews of the work of outstanding new talents

is *The Horn Book*. This invaluable reference for new children's literature is available in most children's libraries. For subscription rates and other information, write to The Horn Book, Inc., 56 Roland St., Suite 200, Boston, MA 02129 or see The Horn Book website: www.hbook.com.

Laughter Holding Both Its Sides. In her classic study, "Children's Poetry Preferences," published in 1974, Ann Terry discovered that humorous poetry topped the list of children's preferences. Guys Read (www. guysread.com), Jon Scieszka's literacy initiative for boys, is an effort to connect boys who don't read much with books that will make them want to read more. "Kids are the best judge of the poetry they like," says Scieszka. But he mentions in a flyer describing Guys Read what he believes is likely to tempt reluctant readers: the funny poetry of Douglas Florian, Colin McNaughton, Jack Prelutsky, and Shel Silverstein.

The teachers in the poetry class bring favorites to class for a hilarious sharing session of humorous verse. They will already have met some of these authors earlier. Especially apt here is the work of Brod Bagert, Hilaire Belloc, John Ciardi, William Cole, Kali Dakos, Douglas Florian, X. J. Kennedy, Dennis Lee, Edward Lear, Phyllis McGinley, Ogden Nash, Jack Prelutsky, Dr. Seuss, Shel Silverstein, and Judith Viorst.

Once in a while in the poetry class a teacher will ask, "But how do you teach these funny poems?" This is a delicate question but an important one. The answer: You don't teach funny poems or *any* poems in a traditional question-and-answer mode. You don't teach facts about poetry. You don't teach *about* poetry.

What you do is trust poetry to do the teaching; after all, it has the words for it. Learning involves experiencing many dozens of poems, delighting in how they use language, and discovering how they work. Learning continues in tentatively trying to write one's own poems.

Over the years, the teachers in my poetry class report that the best questions to use with poetry are the children's own.

CONDUCTING AN AUTHOR STUDY

By this time in the semester, students are ready to choose one poet, after browsing in the works of many, for an author study (see Figure 2.2 for an example). As they continue to read widely, they also begin to concentrate on their chosen poet's works. They read all they can of this poet, taking notes, preparing to be able to generalize, with examples, about the chosen poet's body of work: themes, characteristic style, influences. Teachers in the class, who use their own author studies as models for their children's

> "It seemed to Dorothy [wife and collaborator] and me that children enjoy looking at things close up. They like to see how a machine works, like to see an animal at close range. If they like to inspect things closely and see how they work, why could children not apply this curiosity to poetry?" (X. J. Kennedy in Copeland, 1993/1994, p. 88)

work, find this an excellent research project for upper elementary and middle school students.

The author study has focus and purpose. The work meets the New York State Standards requirements, spanning work in more than one genre: poetry and exposition. Extensive research requires selection, analysis, and organization of material. Oral and written language is involved (writing a report and delivering an oral version of it).

Speaking of Poets, Volumes I and II (Copeland, 1993/1994) are useful references in preparing author studies, as is the Internet. Many poets have their own websites. Scholastic Publishing Company maintains a site featuring poets and other writers. Below is a selected list of websites.

1. www.art-arena.com/poems.htm
   Poems and biographical notes on poets around the world.
2. www.ucalgary.ca/~dkbrown/index/html
   A children's literature web guide.
3. www.scholastic.com
   Poetry exercises and activities; introductions to poets and authors.
4. www.potatohill.com
   Features a poem of the week and creative teaching ideas.

EXAMPLE OF AN AUTHOR STUDY

DOUGLAS FLORIAN
by Lisa Irom

In *Poetry Rules* on www.amazon.com, Douglas Florian wrote: "When I write a poem, I spell words wrong on purpose, use bad grammar, and invent new words. I do all this to make my poems better. That's called poetic license." Florian's use of poetic license enables him to create poems that make adults and children of all ages grin, laugh, and appreciate poetry.

Douglas Florian was born March 18, 1950 in Queens, New York. He studied art at both Queens College, City University of New York and the School of Visual Arts in New York City. A city lover, he lives today in Jamaica, Queens with his wife and five children and works in a studio in Manhattan.

Before Florian published his own works, he drew cartoons and illustrated articles for both *The New Yorker* and *The New York Times*. He illustrated books written by other authors, but soon found it more creative and satisfying to create both text and illustrations. He wrote and illustrated a series of books on various occupations. But he found his true literary niche in writing and illustrating his own poems, making liberal use of poetic license in ways that remind readers of the playful wittiness of Ogden Nash.

Bing, Bang, Boing (1994) is a collection of zany poems that delights young children with its foolishness. *Beast Feast* (1994), won an International Reading Award (1996). *In the Swim* (1997) and *Insectlopedia* (1998) combine actual scientific facts with witty poetic descriptions and free-form paintings of creatures who fly, swim, and crawl. Here is "The Oysters."

"Did you know the ocean's oysters
Sometimes change from girls to boysters?
Then the boys change back to girls.
(Are the girls the ones with pearls?)
(*In the Swim*, p. 42).

Douglas Florian began to draw when he was very young; from the start his art reflected his love of nature. His father taught him to enjoy nature in all its forms; animals and other creatures were the subjects of his early artwork. He credits a Queens College professor, Marvin Bileck, for fostering his skills and offering him encouragement. Delight and inspiration came from encounters with William Cole's collections of humorous poetry.

Douglas Florian is, in his work, silly and funny, but he is also witty and wise. Besides writing about nature, he writes on topics of special interest to young readers, such as school and sports. All of his poems are filled with vitality and good humor. His use of "poetic license" gives his work a sense of fun and playfulness. He believes in writing about what pleases you most. His advice to poetry writers: "Don't be a scaredy-cat when writing poetry. Have fun, break a few rules, and remember: Poetry is great! Poetry rules!"

LEARNING ABOUT POETRY
FROM THE POEMS THEMSELVES

Besides getting to know the poets and their works, the students learn throughout the semester about the genre itself. This is accomplished by means of an inductive process of observation and inquiry, *not* through the deductive learning process wherein learners absorb by rote what *others* have discovered about poetic form. Experiencing poems and responding personally to them always comes before any analysis. As Georgia Heard (1999) warns, "The problem with studying the tools and craft that make a poem work is that because they are the most tangible, logical, and concrete parts of poetry, it's tempting to remain there, ignoring the less tangible meaning that is at the heart of the poem—and is its life" (p. 62).

Investigating how poetry is made leads directly to the writing of it. Every class session contains writing workshop time. One requirement for the course (ungraded but essential for the grade) is a slim volume of original verse.

Inquiry Not Inquisition

One objective of the poetry class is to proceed in ways that can and ought to be replicated in elementary and middle school classrooms. The goal for poetry study in those classrooms is to motivate—not murder— interest and delight in poetry. Accordingly, we let the poems themselves do the teaching. Poetry is *the* language art, after all. In it language ideally is used to greatest effect. We remember that *immersion* was our key word from the beginning. We can't appreciate poetry and we certainly can't attempt to write it without experiencing quantities of it.

We concentrate on poems that interest our specific group. That means we won't impose adult standards on children's choices when we transfer the content of the college poetry class to the children. Taste and critical ability are developed, in any case, through contact with poems at all levels, from excellent to appalling. We aim for variety. Of course, the children love Shel Silverstein's work, and no wonder. But he has scores of colleagues whose names may not be as well known but whose work is just as worthwhile to know.

As to *study* of poetry with elementary and middle school students, we have found that too much intellectualizing too soon leads to groans when poetry time is announced in classrooms. We follow instead Eve Merriam's advice:

> Start light. Give children the whole spectrum. Just relax. There are only two rules for poetry: A poem must be read aloud once for the sense or nonsense; then it must be read aloud for the music. Read, enjoy, then talk about the poem. Do away with questions. Examine the poem instead, reading and re-reading bits of it in turn, picking out words that start the same or sound alike. (cited in Sloan, 1981, p.960)

We take Merriam's expert advice seriously in the class, using this example, in her own words, of good teaching.

Take, for instance, my poem "Lullaby:" (Merriam, 1973).
   sh   sh   what do you wish
   sh   sh   the windows are shuttered
   sh   sh   a magical fish

   swims out from the window and down to the river
   lap   lap   the waters are lapping
   sh   sh   the shore slips away
   glide   glide   glide with the current
   sh   sh   the shadows are deeper
   sleep   sleep   tomorrow is sure

For children to count how many times the sound *sh* is in the poem, they will have to hear the poem read aloud. Just looking at the printed page doesn't give you the sound *sh* found in the word *sure*. Nor is the *sh* always at the beginning of a word; you can hear it in *wish* and *fish*, if you read the poem *out loud*. (cited in Sloan, 1981, p. 960, emphasis in original)

We don't read to answer factual questions about the content of a poem; we certainly don't try to translate a poem into prose in a mistaken effort to get at its "true meaning." We don't read to extract examples of figures of speech; in fact, we assiduously avoid any form of verse vivisection, as Professor Leland Jacobs called the deplorable practice of ransacking poems for poetic devices. We read to enjoy. We read to internalize the linguistic and imaginative marvels poetry contains. And we read to discover for ourselves how poetry works.

Discovering How Poetry Works

Admittedly, it helps if teachers have some understanding of poetic technique as they guide the students' observation and inquiry.

Useful Sources on Poetic Techniques. Myra Cohn Livingston's (1991) invaluable little book, *Poem-Making*, a short course in itself, offers accessible information about poetic techniques. Under "The Voices of Poetry," Livingston defines and discusses lyrical, narrative, and dramatic voice, the latter including apostrophe (a voice addressing something that cannot answer), mask (speaking as someone other than yourself), and conversation. "Sound and Rhyme" deals with couplets, tercets, quatrains, longer stanzas, and the ballad; later, she covers additional forms like haiku, cinquain, limerick, free verse, and others. "Other Elements of Sound" considers repetition, alliteration, onomatopoeia, off rhyme, consonance, and assonance. There is discussion of rhythm and metrics and figures of

---

Figure 2.2. Readings on Poetry

Chukofsky, K. (1963). *From two to five* (translated and edited by Miriam Morton). Berkeley: University of California Press.

A classic by the Russian poet. Discusses why poetry is the natural language of children.

Esbensen, B. J. (1995). *A celebration of bees: Helping children to write poetry.* New York: Henry Holt.

Winner of the NCTE Poetry Award. Offers advice on helping children to write poetry.

Heard, G. (1989). *For the good of the earth and the sun: Teaching poetry.*

Heard, G. (1999). *Awakening the heart.* Portsmouth, NH: Heinemann.

Poet Georgia Heard shares her experiences presenting poetry and helping children to write poetry in New York City schools. Readers find her readable books both inspiring and practical, offering especially valuable advice on how to coach children as they write poetry.

Kennedy, X. J., & Kennedy, D. (1982). *Knock at a star: A child's introduction to poetry.* Boston: Little, Brown.

An anthology of good poems selected by a poet. Helpful comment on the poems is included.

Janeczko, P. (1999). *How to write poetry.* New York: Scholastic.

Models and exercises to engage children in poetry-writing.

Oliver, M. (1994). *A poetry handbook.* New York: Harcourt Brace.

Winner of both the Pulitzer Prize and the National Book Award, Oliver discusses the basics of poetry writing.

---

speech. Other excellent beginning books on poetry and how poetry is made are listed in Figure 2.2.

Discovering Form Through the Poems. By far the best way to discover how poetry works is to look closely at poems. "Tell me anything you notice about the *form* of the poems you've been reading," I say to the students. "How are they constructed?" These are some of the insights of adult students, with examples.

> *"Poems can be a series of questions; sometimes, they are built up of a question and an answer or answers."*

Does the restless sea grow weary?
Does it long to lie still and rest?
Does it tire of cries of sea birds?
Does it seek an end to its quest?

What do you see in the clouds drifting by?
I've seen lambs with wind-tossed wool,
Once a spiny-backed dragon breathing fire,
Today a two-headed monster on a throne,
Yesterday a forest of mushroom trees,
A monster cow with a triple horn,
A pup, a cup, a long-beaked bird, a lyre.

> *"A poem, especially if it is unrhymed, can be a statement, long or short."*

Arranged on a staff of high wires
In twos and fours,
Birds perch, round black silhouettes
Against the sky,
Composing bird song.

> *"Poems are often lists."*

Favorite books of mine?
Wild Things and Madeline,
Peter, Cat in the Hat, Nate the Great,
Goodnight Moon when I was small
Frog and Toad, The Big Orange Splot,
Dozens more, with a little thought.

> *"Lots of poems are made up of groups of two or more rhymed lines."*

The reference here is to two–line couplets and four–line quatrains. In couplets, lines are usually approximately the same length. Quatrains can have many different rhyme schemes: *aabb*, *abab*, *abba*, *abcb*, and so on. The line length of quatrains may vary, with lines 1 and 3 having eight syllables; lines 2 and 4, six syllables. There is flexibility in line length and no hard-and-fast rules.

Couplet

A brown doe stepped from the forest into the roadway ahead,
Saw me stare, came toward me a step, stopped, then fled.

Quatrain

Stopping near the old stone fence
I looked into a chipmunk's eyes,
Saw tiny beads of polished jet
Regard me with surprise.

"*Longer poems that tell stories [ballads] may be composed of a series of quatrains.*"

In days of yore from shore to shore
Evil spirits ruled the land,
Killed knights and ladies by the droves,
Ruled with a mighty hand.

Then giants in shining armor came;
Their weapons were their brains.
They battled fierce the evil force
Until they held the reins.

The first and bravest knight who rode
Was Louis Pasteur by name;
He slew the wicked anthrax germ,
And justly earned his fame.

A scourge that spread and killed its prey
Was smallpox, full of dread;
The strength of Edward Jenner's sword
Slew that enemy dead.

As the battle rose and raged,
Two heroes, Banting and Best
Arose and conquered the cursed foe;
Diabetes was laid to rest.

The enemy polio that crippled and maimed
For many a dread-filled year,
Was conquered by the determined Salk;
Our debt to him is clear.

Another curse by Koch laid low,
Though it put up a mighty fight,

Was tuberculosis, tough and strong;
But now its end's in sight.

The strongest foe we've met thus far,
Whose end is still being sought,
Is cancer with cells that grow and spread;
This battle is still being fought.

These shining knights in armor white
Have fought a fight that's worth
More than all the treasure and wealth
That we'll ever find on earth.

—Judy Wendeborn, eighth–grade student

"Some poems have specific patterns of syllables, like the haiku with 17 arranged 5, 7, 5, or the cinquain, an unrhymed poem of five lines with 2, 4, 6, 8, and 2 syllables respectively."

Haiku

I wonder who thought
Of having a little bug
Carry a night light.

Cinquain

The form
Of the cinquain
Is precise, and its lines,
Unrhymed, must flow, a stream of words,
As here.

Since most teachers love to talk and especially to ask questions, they at first find it difficult to let go, to let poetry do much of the teaching. But when they discover that experiencing and exploring poetry *with* their students is far more effective teaching than quizzing and questioning *about* poetry, they are relieved, although perhaps a little guilty to find that teaching and learning can be so pleasurable.

The teachers begin to acknowledge the significance of these words of Eve Merriam: "If we can get teachers to read poetry, lots of it, out loud to children, we'll develop a generation of poetry readers; we may even have some poetry writers. But the main thing, we'll have language appreciators" (cited in Sloan, 1981, p. 960).

True literacy begins in appreciation of written words.

CHAPTER 3

Writer's Workshop

Most sessions of the college poetry class include time for writing. What follows are some of the exercises we undertake, often in small groups or with partners. This chapter includes a sampling of forms and approaches to writing poetry, with examples from college students, children, and the author.

RIDDLES: BEGINNING AT THE BEGINNING

An early lesson in the poetry class involves an exercise in riddling, which can be as successful with children as with adults. We begin poetry writing with riddles because the riddle is among the most ancient of poetic forms. In riddles, things are described in terms of other things, as in this old one whose answer is a bell.

> As round as an apple,
> As deep as a pail:
> It never cries out
> Till it's caught by the tail.

Nineteenth-century French poet Mallarmé's prescription for writing poetry—to describe, not the thing, but the effect it produces—is essentially an instruction for creating a riddle. The riddler and the poet think alike, declaring that A is like B, even that A *is* B. These categories, similarity and identification, we know in poetry as simile and metaphor.

In small groups, students examine an object such as a paper clip, a key, a battery, a crayon. Their task is to *describe not the object itself but the effect it produces*; in other words, to say, as the poet often does, *what the object is like*. The group composes a riddle, which can rhyme as does this ancient one describing the fog:

A house full, a hole full,
But you cannot gather a bowl full.

The riddle may be less direct, may employ literary allusions, and may not rhyme, as in this example from a group in the college class whose object was an apple seed:

From my growth
Came Eve's downfall,
And from it will come
Health without doctors.

College students created this riddle about a balloon:

Aloft in color, I am a planet
To young eyes; Pale,
I am the sailing moon.

Imagery is at the heart of a good poem, alongside rhythm and sound. Practicing riddling, describing something in terms of something unlike yet *imaginatively* alike, teachers have found is one way to coax fresh images from children. Speaking of the wind and a pencil, respectively, elementary students wrote: "I am the earth's breath, heard, but not seen." "Ideas line up behind my pointed end, waiting to squeeze through."

A marble and a book inspired these lines from a student:

Marble

Though I have a rainbow
inside me,
I'm a ball with no bounce
and children push me around.

Pencil

I am speechless
Yet full of words.

A battery and an earring spurred graduate students to write:

Battery

A magician?
More a deity.

I cause the light.
I draw music from the air.
I bring the dead to life.

Earring

This ring fits no finger,
Encircles no finger,
Encircles no thing.

In this exercise, there is no requirement to rhyme unless the riddlers wish to riddle in rhyme. Riddling requires, most of all, use of vivid imagery, often through metaphor and simile. Pun, personification, repetition, and apostrophe (directly addressing an inanimate object or a creature who cannot answer) can be useful in creating a riddle. Employing these poetic devices, without rhyme, makes the riddle writing an exercise in free verse.

On the other hand, it is fun to attempt rhyming riddles, especially couplets, in the manner of J. Patrick Lewis (1996, 1998b) and Charles Chigna (1995). This rhyme is about a Siamese cat:

Smooth brown mound,
Tail around.
Up. Bound.
Not a sound.

READ TO WRITE

According to the teachers in my classes, a sure way to turn children off from poetry is to suddenly give the order: "Write a poem," or worse, "Write a poem, at home tonight or over the weekend. Any subject you want." Classroom stories of success with poetry writing seldom if ever begin with these words. Success stories do begin with *reading* poetry, lots of it, with no strings of questions attached. It's safe to say that every successful writer of poetry was first a reader of quantities of it.

Success means sufficient familiarity with poetry to *notice* things about its construction. Of course, teachers may need to guide this noticing with careful choice of poems for presentation. But the secret to success is always familiarity with large numbers of poems. Then comes inquiry.

"Look closely at these poems we've read," a teacher might say to her second grade, referring to a sheaf of poems printed on chart paper on the easel. "Look at the words. Let's read them aloud. What do you notice about them?"

Someone may notice, if the teacher has chosen her examples with care, that the last words in pairs of lines (couplets) share the same sound (rhyme), that the first sound in many words is the same (alliteration), that some of the words sound like the thing they're describing (onomatopoeia). Teaching the names of the poetic devices is optional; what is important is that the children discover, from their experiences with poetry, how poetic devices work.

"I don't think it's wrong to tell students about simile, metaphor, and personification," says Georgia Heard (1989), "but the explanations should have an organic origin. . . . Taught out of context, without an understanding of how poets use them, the labels become another way to turn students off to poetry—to make them yawn at the mention of the word" (p. 69).

FREEDOM THROUGH FORM

Certain beliefs have grown up like weeds around the subject of poetry writing. My students' classroom experiences make them adamant in disagreement with at least two of these prevalent notions. The first, to be found in commercial language arts workbooks and other dark places, and one that most teachers found inhibited their children, is that poetry must "express your deepest feelings." Of course, some poetry does. But much of it, particularly that intended for children, does not. Many poems and verses, particularly those beloved by children, exist for their sound or their nonsense, not for their sense at all. Where is the outpouring of deep emotion in this marvelous nonsense of Edward Lear's "The Quangle Wangle's Hat" (Jackson, 1951)?

> And the Golden Grouse came there
> And the Pobble who has no toes
> And the small Olympian bear
> And the Dong with the luminous nose.
> And the Blue Baboon
> Who played the flute
> And the Orient Calf from the land of Tute
> And the Attery Squash and the Bisky bat
>
> All came and built on the lovely hat
> Of the Quangle Wangle Quee. (pp. 253–254)

"You don't necessarily have to work the 'fancy' into the poem or have an unhappy life to write about the fullness of life and everything in it" (Cynthia Rylant in Copeland, 1994, p. 30).

Of course, what we write must be *meaningful* to us or it isn't worth the trouble of writing. And what we write will be grounded in our experience: something we saw or felt or did. The objective, says Myra Cohn Livingston (1991), is to write so "our listeners and readers can sense something of what we have encountered, see something they have never noticed before, or look at something in a fresh way; . . . we hope to make the image, the thought, even the sound come alive again" (p. x).

Poet and teacher Georgia Heard (1999) speaks often about helping children to sift through the layers of their lives in search of their own truths and their own poems. This is a worthy quest, because we want young poets to write honest poems. Referring to Howard Gardner's multiple intelligences, Heard (1999) makes the point that reading and writing poetry is the key to knowing and managing one's feelings, to *emotional* literacy, an intelligence often neglected.

The second nefarious notion is that asking children to write in a specific form kills their creativity. Over the years, no teachers in my poetry class have supported this idea. In their experience, forms free, rather than curtail, the freedom to create. Left on their own with the instruction: Write a poem, all but exceptionally literary children are at a loss.

The famous patterns developed by Kenneth Koch (1970) for writing about wishes, lies, and dreams meet with success today as they did when he used them first with the students of P.S. 61 in New York City. The "wish" poem begins with "I wish." Every line contains a color, a comic strip character, and a city or country: "I wish I was Dick Tracy in a black suit in England" (p. 6). Another Koch pattern based on the notion of "then and now" is I used to be—But now I am—. Example: "I used to have a hat of hearts but now I have a hat of tears" (p. 166).

Many of the children in my students' classes are very young; large numbers speak and write English as a second language. Both in reading and writing poetry, they will begin with baby steps and plenty of support. Writing two-word poems, or terse verse, as Bruce McMillan calls it in his photo essay, *One Sun* (1990), is a major achievement for many.

Although we are well aware that poetry doesn't always have to rhyme, we also know, from our exploration of poetry, that most poetry written for children *does* rhyme. Furthermore, our collective experience over the years informs us that children prefer rhymed over so-called free verse. This is not to say that we won't introduce children to the unique beauties of fine unrhymed verse. In most cases, however, teachers won't begin with it.

Of course, there is danger in rhyming. Children often stretch sense to make a rhyme. The challenge is to rhyme well and make sense. This takes time and thought and perhaps the assistance of a rhyming dictionary. As David McCord (1962) says, speaking in one of his books as the poetry coach, Professor Brown:

> A couplet is two lines—two lines in rime.
> The first comes easy, the second may take time. (p. 49)

A SAMPLER OF POETIC FORMS

Couplets

After riddles, teachers work with the forms the children discover from their reading and listening to poems. Many poems are made up of couplets, two rhyming lines, both with approximately the same number of syllables. First-grade children in the Bronx wrote couplets about themselves (always a topic of interest for any poet):

> William says he likes to skateboard,
> When he does, he won't get bored.

> How are you? My name's Miguel;
> I love math and do it well.

> Jasmine, a perfume, is my name
> But I like it all the same.

Triplets

A triplet is three lines of approximately the same length with various rhyme schemes, but most often *aba*. For topics, look to literature, or the social studies or science curriculum.

> Christopher Columbus, sails unfurled
> On three small ships in 1492
> Came to change forever this New World

> "It has always seemed to me curious that the instruction of poetry has followed a path different from the courses of study intended to develop talent in the field of music or the visual arts, where a step-by-step learning process is usual. . . . The intention is not to accomplish a bona fide act of creation, but is an example of what must necessarily come first—exercise." (Mary Oliver, 1994, p. 2)

Ballads

The ballad is a series of quatrains that tell a story. Teachers have found that older children enjoy the challenge of recasting material, such as a story in prose, in ballad form or using the form to write a book report or an account of an historical incident. Here is the first stanza from graduate student Angela Pagnozzi's "book report" on a famous story:

The Ballad of the Wild Things

One mischievous evening, a boy named Max
Donned his wolf suit and began to attack
His room, his house, and his cute little pup.
He told his mother,"I'll eat you all up."

A family story or favorite tale may be retold effectively as a ballad. In the college poetry class, students labor lovingly over the ballads they include in their slim volume of original verse, meeting the challenge of telling a story, including dialogue, and writing lines that scan. One student worked all term revising and reworking her ballad on the story of Esther, the Biblical heroine. The following is the work of Janice Gordon, another student in the graduate poetry class:

In a small neighborhood called Little Neck,
Where fat black cables stretched deck to deck,
All the children hated to go to school;
But watching TV, they agreed, was cool.

Every day after three o'clock,
Not a single child would play on the block;
Indoors they'd sit in flickering light,
Never turning their heads to left or right.

Their faces turned a ghostly white,
Their clothes became a little tight.
They never played ball or swam in the pool;
Just watching TV, they agreed, was cool.

Trying to drag them away from the screen,
Parents longed for the way things had been;
"We miss how they'd play with sister and brother;
We even miss times when they'd fight each other."

The teachers in Public School 94
Hardly recalled how it had been before
When children focused on reading and math.
"We'd be happy," they cried, "If they just took a bath!"

It's true; the classrooms grew quite smelly,
For kids did nothing but look at the telly.
Dinner they ate from a little snack table;
They cared not for food, but only for cable.

Years passed. Lazy children turned into slobs
Who did nothing but turn a few knobs.
They couldn't read, so of course couldn't vote.
Their choices were only made by remote.

Without any readers, just turners of knobs,
There were no people to do any jobs,
No one to govern and make decisions,
Boil an egg or repair televisions.

Little by little, TV's bit the dust,
Cables corroded, closed circuits went bust.
"What will become of us?" tube viewers cried.
The answer is easy. They sat till they died.

Rhythmic Repetitions: Catalogues and Lists

The sonorous repetitive rhythms of the Bible supply powerful patterns
to examine and try to emulate.

From Psalm 150

Praise ye the Lord
Praise God in his sanctuary:
Praise him in the firmament of his power.

"One of the most difficult things about writing a poem is finding the right form. . . . One of my students decided to write a poem about television. He tried couplets, tercets, quatrains, a ballad, a haiku, a cinquain, free verse, a shape poem, and even more. Some worked out very well. Others were all wrong." (Myra Cohn Livingston, 1991, p. 103).

> Praise him for his mighty acts:
> Praise him according to his excellent greatness.
> Praise him with the sound of the trumpet:
> Praise him with the psaltry and harp.
> Praise him with the timbrel and dance.

In list and catalogue poems, repetition is a feature. The poem may be rhymed or unrhymed. Variation in line length adds rhythm. To add interest, poetic devices such as alliteration may be employed. The writer needs to work toward vivid imagery. A holiday or holy day can be the inspiration for such a poem, the teacher offering a starting phrase as primer: "Let us be thankful for . . . " This is a form that can be adapted for use with the youngest children, the teacher taking dictation on a chart or chalkboard. The familiar song, "These Are a Few of My Favorite Things," provides a good model for a list poem.

Acrostics

This simple form, rhymed or unrhymed, may use a name, a holy day, or holiday as subject. Varying the line lengths adds rhythm. Lines may rhyme or not. The letters of the acrostic word need not appear at the beginning of each line but may be embedded within the lines, an even greater challenge to the writer.

> I have traveled thousands of miles to
> Make my new home in a strange land.
> Missing all the familiar places of my childhood,
> I feel at first a stranger to myself,
> Grown shy, red-faced, searching for words
> Restless, longing only to return to
> All I have left behind. But No!

No, I tell myself, Look ahead, however hard
To leave the past. Live here and now.

Chants and Prayers

A chant or prayer often addresses the Deity. It uses repetition and usually asks or entreats. This Pueblo medicine song is an example:

Now bring the Corn, Our Mother,
Bring the life-giving Corn
In all our thoughts and words
Let us do only good;
In all our acts and words
Let us be all as one.

Alphabet Poem

These are good exercises for groups. The idea is to work through the alphabet; the challenge is to make sense and to employ imagery and other poetic devices, such as alliteration, and perhaps internal rhyme.

A
Blue jay
Came fluttering
Down,
Every
Feather
Glowing in the sunshine.
He, cocky one,
Installed himself
Just there, atop the feeder,
Kinglike.
Little chickadees
Milled about
Nearby, twittering, as if to say:
Our
Private time is
Quite over—over—unless we
Rush this bully and
Send him flying.
Tuft held
Up like a crown, the blue
Villain suddenly declared

"Trying out pattern poetry can be fun. One of the problems, however, is that oftentimes we let the shapes work so hard—place so much attention on the art—that words become secondary." (Myra Cohn Livingston, 1991, p. 146)

War on chickadees. Putting on
Xtra power to scatter the black caps
Yet again, he dived
ZOOM! And they fled.

Shape Poetry

Concrete or shape poetry uses words to fill in or outline a shape. Words may describe the shape in creative ways or use repetition for effect. A ruler, for instance, might be made up entirely of the word inch.

inch
inch
inch
inch
inch
inch
inch
inch
inch
inch
inch
inch

Douglas Florian (1997) cleverly shapes a sawfish in words, as shown in Figure 3.1.

Cinquain and Haiku

Cinquain and haiku are perhaps the most common forms used in classrooms, but they are not always well served there. We have found it not advisable to start poetry writing with them. Although they appear simple, good ones are neither simplistic nor easy to create.

Figure 3.1. Douglas Florian shapes a sawfish in words.

The Sawfish

You'll see a saw

Upon my jaw,

But I can't cut

A two-by-four,

Or build a bed,

Or frame a door

My splendid saw's

For goring fishes

I eat them raw

And don't do dishes.

The haiku, a form that originated in Japan, is a three-line "snapshot" or reflection, most often about nature. Although the form need not be rigidly followed, it is usual to keep close to the pattern of 5, 7, 5 syllables. Children should be entreated not to make banal statements and call them haiku. Instead, before they attempt to write their own, they should experience as many fine examples of the form as possible.

Basho was a beloved poet of Japan. His haiku may be sampled in a book about his life: *Grass Sandals: The Travels of Basho* (Spivak, 1997). Born in 1763 in Japan, another revered writer of haiku is Issa, whose life story and poems are presented for children in *Cool Melons—Turn to Frogs! The Life and Poems of Issa* (Gollub, 1998).

Cinquain, a form developed in the twentieth century by Adelaide Crapsey, a young American poet, means "a grouping of five." Unrhymed, the true cinquain follows a specific construction of five lines of 2, 4, 6, 8, 2 *syllables*, respectively. There is another format—two words for title, four words describing the title, six words with an action relating to the title, eight

"Writing haiku is not easy. It is really the hardest kind of poem I know of to write well. . . . A true cinquain is a form in which we are not concerned with parts of speech; rather, we try to express ourselves in some image or thought. . . . The twenty-two syllable pattern is just long enough" (Myra Cohn Livingston, 1991, p. 112).

words expressing a feeling about the title, and two words to express the title in another way—perhaps developed in the mistaken belief that children are incapable of learning to count syllables, but it is not a cinquain at all and should be avoided. Misinterpretation of haiku and cinquain often results in the committing of banalities unworthy of young poets.

David McCord's Professor Brown teaches the proper form of the cinquain in his book of verse, *For Me to Say* (1970). Here is an excerpt:

This is
The form of the
Cinquain. The five lines have
2, 4, 6, 8, 2 syllables
As here. (p. 93)

Septone

The septone is seven lines of simple, just-for-fun unrhymed verse based on one's own (or someone else's) phone number. The number of syllables (or words, if you prefer) in each line is dictated by the phone number. Eighth grader Matthew Zdebiak created the following septone from 627–4446:

I like to play hockey
I like
The excitement of the game.
As I suit up,
I wish and hope
My team will win
And I will score four goals.

Apostrophe

In this form, an inanimate object, or something that cannot answer, is addressed in a rhymed or unrhymed poem.

Forget-me-not,
Tiny flower, petals small,
Hardly there at all,
Did you know
They've named
A color after you?
It's true.
Not robin's egg blue,
Not Wedgwood, nor French,
Not periwinkle. No.
But the best of the lot:
The blue of a June sky
To the power of ten,
The true blue of
Forget-me-not.

Definition Poetry

The word to be defined begins the poem in a question; the rest of the poem answers the question.

What is prayer?
A quiet time,
Time to reflect,
A time to listen
For the still voice
That offers peace.
Prayer: your time
With the Deity on
A private line.

Limerick

The limerick is a challenging form, for it is written with precise rhythm. One needs to hear many examples out loud before attempting to write it. Perhaps the most famous examples are the works of Edward Lear (1991), the nineteenth-century king of craziness in words.

There was an old man in a Marsh
Whose manners were futile and harsh;
He sate on a log, and sang songs to a frog,
That instructive old man in a Marsh.

There was a young lady whose nose
Was so long that it reached to her toes;
So she hired an Old Lady, whose conduct was steady,
To carry that wonderful nose.

There was an Old Man with a beard,
Who said, "It is just as I feared!—
Two Owls and a Hen, four Larks and a Wren,
Have all built their nests in my beard!"

Free Verse

"Free verse is not, of course, free," writes award-winning poet Mary Oliver (1994). "It is free from formal metrical design, but it certainly isn't free from some kind of design. Is poetry language that is spontaneous, impulsive? Yes, it is. It is also language that is composed, considered, appropriate, and effective" (p. 67).

Free verse is a relatively recent form. Poets began writing free verse at the beginning of the twentieth century, perhaps in an effort to make poetic expression less formal and measured, closer to people's way of speaking. Teachers have found that a good recipe for free verse is this: Take the correct form of the cinquain, arrived at by counting syllables; choose a topic, any topic; add vivid images and other poetic devices like alliteration; work toward a smooth flow of words from line to line; avoid end rhymes.

This attempt at free verse was a group effort in 1999 by Ms. Regina Corpus's fourth grade in P.S. 92 Manhattan.

My New York

My New York is
Famous
Beautiful buildings:
The Empire State Building,
The Twin Towers,
The Chrysler Building,
Diamonds in the night.
My New York is
Traffic jams,
Sirens wailing, signaling
Trouble is near.
My New York

> "Robert Frost has said that writing free verse is like playing tennis without a net. Other poets would agree with him that to work within set patterns offers a challenge, helps us to work harder and better toward a good poem. But many poets today feel that metrics or old forms are too confining and do not express the tempo of our life" (Myra Cohn Livingston, 1991, p. 127).

Gives my nose
Plenty of scents:
Barbeque, flowers, hot dogs, and pretzels,
Roasting chestnuts, pizza, smog
Bakeries, Chinese take-out,
And coffee.
My New York
Is charged with energy:
People rushing to and fro,
Fast trains underground,
Buses honking at tricky taxi cabs.
See. Hear, Sniff for yourself.
Visit
My New York.

Speaking of group efforts: Teachers strongly support these in writing workshops in their classrooms. They also advocate brainstorming words and phrases before writing and the creation of a "word wall" that will help poets as they strike out on their own.

WORDS OF CAUTION

Myths and superstitions abound in education. One is the persistent idea that form inhibits creativity in writing. Another is the notion that even the kindliest pushes toward perfecting their work discourage children. Our work in classrooms proves both of these to be untrue. Accepting their banal statements as poetry does children no favor. They aren't fooled. They know they can do better, given the chance. Rushing through an assignment is a recipe for weak work; good writing requires time and thought.

Poets who participated in a Poetry Institute organized by members of the International Reading Association's Special Interest Group for Reading and Children's Literature at the IRA's Annual Convention in New Orleans, 2001.

Joan Graham:
"One of the best parts of writing poetry is surprising yourself–each poem is an act of discovery."

Eloise Greenfield:
"It's the musicality of a poem that is the magnet, drawing us into the exploration of ideas and emotions."

Alice Schertle:
"Two words for anyone who wants to write poetry: 'Read Poetry!'"

Avis Harley:
"Celebrate poetry– that love of word: the written, the read, the spoken, the heard."

Janet Wong:
"Poetry is the word-version of a photograph, capturing time and movement in a rhythmic frame."

Brod Bagert:
"Poetry is a happy life."

Pat Mora:
"Poetry is playing with words, the private pleasure of hearing them begin to sing."

Kristine O'Connell George:
"Poetry is only a handful of words–yet somehow these words can vibrate with a passion that cannot be ignored or forgotten."

From author studies, children learn that writers seldom publish first drafts, that they labor over even the briefest poems through many revisions. Children learn from experience that their own work can be improved by selecting another word here, by describing more precisely there, by thinking of a comparison for "white," say, or "soft," that isn't a tired cliché.

RESOURCES ON POETIC FORMS

Required reading for the poetry course at Queens College includes two books by poet and teacher Georgia Heard: *For the Good of the Earth and the Sun* (1989) and *Awakening the Heart* (1999). Heard's pages are filled with dozens of practical suggestions for bringing children and poetry together. But, to teachers, she is most impressive when she describes how she coaches children as they write poetry, drawing from them their best work, refusing to let them be dull and mediocre.

Here is a sampling of her good advice in *Awakening the Heart*.

> Are there words or lines that sound awkward, that clink on the page? What words or lines sound strong, pleasing, "poetic," or memorable? Are there any words or lines that sound stale or clichéd? Does the poem make you feel anything? Which words, lines, or images move you most? Is the poem clear or does it feel confused? Can you see the images in the poem? Are they clear, powerful, concrete, vivid? . . . What words, images, rhythms, or thoughts catch you by surprise—give you that ahhh! feeling? (pp. 119–120)

There are many other resources you might use or adapt for use with children of all ages. A good general reference is the expanded second edition of *Handbook of Poetic Forms,* edited by poet Ron Padgett (2000). Although the book is intended for adults, its content may be adapted for use in elementary and middle school classrooms. The 77 entries, each with a definition and examples, are arranged alphabetically beginning with abstract poem, allegory, and going all the way to terza rima, triolet, and villanelle. In between are intriguing forms like the eclogue, pantoum, rap, renga, rondeau, and sestina

Two other books on poetic form, easily accessible for independent use by children in elementary and middle school, are Avis Harley's *Fly with Me: An ABC of Poetry* (2000) and *Leap into Poetry: More ABCs of Poetry* (2001). The books introduce, with examples and colorful illustrations, a variety of forms and techniques. Unusual forms are represented such as the doublet, chazal, clerihew, quintet, rhopalic verse, sonnet, waka, xcogito, and more.

CHAPTER 4

Poetry Applied

Many teachers—Queens College students—enter my graduate course, Poetry for Children, attracted by a course description that promises knowledge about poetry and its place in classroom programs to develop literacy. In the beginning, few are aware of how rich a resource is available to them and their students in the wide range of verse and poetry written especially for children. Sadly, many arrive wary of all things poetic, recalling from high school days uncomfortable New Critical encounters with poems.

As we discuss our attitudes toward poetry, these are typical comments: "We were supposed to figure out the hidden meanings in poems, but we always seemed to be wrong." "We took the poem apart word by word until I never wanted to see or hear it again." "I got the idea that you had to have special ability to interpret poems, and I just didn't seem to have it."

Too many teachers endow poetry with a mystique. Those who do are likely to approach it formally, even reverentially. In an interview, Eve Merriam (personal communication, 1981) told me that often her first task in workshops with teachers was to "demystify" poetry for them, to free them to enjoy the nonsense of wordplay, the liveliness of rhythm and rhyme, the puzzle-like challenge of putting poems together. Mindful of this, we set out in the poetry class for a semester of enjoying ourselves with poetry: reading, collecting, sharing, creating. Before long, teachers are marveling at the variety and amount of fine poetry available for children and planning how to bring the poems to the children.

Some teachers report that their students "don't like poetry," find it "boring," "silly," or "only for girls." A little investigation is likely to reveal that these children have only a passing acquaintance with poetry or perhaps have been marked by unpleasant experiences related to poetry. Perhaps they had to listen to poems with absolutely no child appeal; maybe they were subjected to undistinguished or downright incompetent reading. They may have been forced to memorize a poem chosen by a teacher, or required to write a poem with no instruction or examples to guide them, or—worse yet—made to find, list, and define a poem's figures of speech.

CLASSROOM RESEARCH

As an assignment in my poetry course, teachers work to reverse any negative attitudes about poetry their students might have by presenting it in ways that preserve delight and destroy drudgery. They plan how they will remedy limited experience with poetry by encouraging children to discover their own favorites among the thousands of poems by hundreds of poets writing on innumerable subjects. They remedy lack of knowledge about poetry by designing opportunities for children to discover how poems are made and to experiment with making some of their own.

Each teacher designs an exercise in informal classroom "research." This begins with a simple survey to measure the children's knowledge of poetry and attitudes toward it. The teachers create surveys appropriate for their group of children. Prereaders may have questions or statements read aloud to them, responding to each with a drawing of a happy or sad face.

Some statements in the survey are open-ended, such as:

Poetry to me is
Poems make me feel
Writing poetry is
Reading poetry is
Talking about poetry is
These are the kinds of poems I know
My favorite poet is
My favorite poem is

Other items in the survey may be more specific, to be answered Yes or No.

I enjoy reading poetry.
I enjoy listening to poetry.
I enjoy writing poetry.
I enjoy talking about poetry.
I own poetry books.
I check out poetry books from the library.
I read poems mostly in school.

Based on their findings, the teachers design a "treatment," for their classes, a thoughtfully planned program of study that may continue for several days or stretch over many weeks. We have found that, in most cases, the surveys indicate that the children know relatively little about poetry. Often, their attitude toward poetry is unfortunately negative. The study is designed to wipe out ignorance about poetry and change attitudes toward it for the better.

Over many years of teaching this class and assigning this exercise, I, together with the classroom teachers, have discovered, *without exception*, that planned, intensive effort to use poetry in the classroom, even over the short span of a few weeks, has marked results in increased knowledge, changed attitudes, and, to some extent, improvement of language skills— or, at the very least, increased interest in written language. This effort must avoid the abuses recalled by many of my students, including: forced memorization, use of poems of little interest to children, verse vivesection, learning the names of poetic devices and rummaging in poems to find them, and erroneous attempts to get at the "true meaning" of a poem by trying to translate it into prose.

At the end of the "treatment" or program of study, the survey given previously or a slightly altered form of it is administered. Spaces following questions about poets and poetry, left blank on the first survey, now bloom with names of poets and titles of favorite poems. A child who at first wrote, "Poetry is too hard to read" now says, "Poetry is words leaping off the page." In the beginning, few children reported checking out poetry books from the library; now, most report that they often borrow books of poems. Children speak of "learning a lot," of being surprised that poetry could be "so fun."

In the rest of this chapter, I have included excerpts from reports of these projects, undertaken in kindergarten through middle school. These accounts are representative of teachers' experiences repeated over many semesters. *In every case*, teachers learn through this assignment that children and poetry, properly introduced, are natural partners in the development of literacy, which begins with taking an interest in words.

AILEEN KLINGER'S KINDERGARTEN

I have 27 African American children between 5 and 6 years old in my class. Much of my curriculum is organized around thematic units, but I have never included a significant amount of poetry in them.

Since we were planning a visit to a farm, we all agreed that learning about farms was a good idea. I decided to use poetry as the main vehicle

> "When I work with [small children], I never ask them to write a poem. I ask them to write a very simple description of a thing, something they feel something about. They then discover that if written in a poetic form on a page, some of the things that they are writing are really poems because the imagery is so fresh and the rhythm is good" (Karla Kuskin in Copeland, 1993/1994, p. 40).

to teach this unit. I knew that kindergarten children have a wide variety of poetry under their belts in the form of nursery rhymes, jump-rope rhymes, taunt songs, riddles, finger plays, and television jingles. I would use this knowledge and also search for as many poems as I could find that would be age-appropriate, catchy, repetitive, and fun.

Since these children are prereaders, I conducted a very simple and informal oral survey to see what they knew about poetry. I asked if they knew what a poem was. None of the children could answer. Then I asked what their favorite nursery rhyme was. Just about every hand was raised. I made a list of their responses and explained that these were poems and that they did know what poetry was after all. They just didn't know that they knew.

The farm unit was planned for a 2-week period. The first day I wrote the traditional nursery rhyme "Hey Diddle Diddle" on chart paper and we read it together several times. We also performed the traditional call and response poem "Did You Feed My Cow?" and sang "Old MacDonald Had a Farm."

The next day I read a selection of poems about pigs from the handout we received in class [poems on pigs in a variety of forms by Mary Ann Hoberman, Arnold Lobel, Christina Rosetti, Susan Schmeltz, and Valerie Worth]. We sang "Old MacDonald" as we cleaned up our room.

The third day of the unit we got dirty. We made mud! I read poems about mud, including Dennis Lee's (1977) "The Muddy Puddle." We discussed why some farm animals, pigs especially, like mud. As the children played in the mud, they described how it felt to them and I wrote down their responses as a list: dirty, icky, gooey, mushy, slushy, sticky. Then I arranged the words on a chart in the style of a "poem," with white space and repetition.

Mud feels
Icky

Sticky
Mud feels
Gooey
Mud feels
Mushy, Slushy

On the fourth day, I taught the children the song "Oh, Lovely Mud" from the Storybox Read Together Audio Cassettes. I read another mud poem, presented in picture book form; it is a fun book because it tells about and shows all the things that got muddied. On a chart, we listed all the things that got muddied in the story poem. We thought of rhyming words to go with these. They rhymed "box," "rocks," and "fox" with "socks."

The next day I followed the form used in Margaret Wise Brown's *I Like Bugs* (2000) and had the children change the words to create:

I like mud
brown mud
gooey mud
sticky, icky, yucky mud
I like mud.

We practiced "Oh, Lovely Mud" as a round. I tape-recorded their voices and used the taped version for the first round. The children were excited to hear their voices on tape.

The sixth day I reread "Did You Feed My Cow?" with the children responding at appropriate places and pantomiming the actions. We recited "This Little Piggy" and sang "Bingo." I read a limerick, "The Old Man and the Cow" by Edward Lear, several times (by request). The children clapped to the rhythm of the limerick and were able to memorize it easily because of the rereadings and the catchy beat. They loved the sound of the word *limerick*.

The next day we made little books of the nursery rhymes we had learned. I wrote out the texts of the verses and the children illustrated them. Their homework was to "read" aloud from their nursery rhyme "books" to someone at home. This time as we cleaned up, I changed the words of "Old MacDonald" to "Old MacDonald had a room/EIEIO/And every day he cleaned that room/EIEIO/With a sweep, sweep here, A sweep, sweep there . . ."

On the eighth day, I decided to introduce "terse verse" to them. Terse verse is simply two rhyming words; there are good examples of it in Bruce

McMillan's books. I read them some examples, like *One Sun* (1990). Then I gave them examples using the names of farm animals, such as Big Pig. They had fun with this exercise, coming up with Fat Cat, Turkey Lurkey (connecting with a folktale we'd read), Cow Now, Bony Pony.

The next day I reread several of the nursery rhymes we had learned, as the children followed along on the chart. Then we said the verses together. We added "To Market, To Market," "Mary Had a Little Lamb," and "Little Bo Beep." Most of the children already knew these.

I had prepared poetry puzzles beforehand. I wrote the rhymes out with pictures and cut them into puzzle pieces. In groups of four, the children assembled them and read them to one another. They switched groups and read again.

The following day we discussed "rap." Most of the children knew what it was. As a special surprise, my assistant and I performed the story of the three little pigs set to a rap rhythm. The children loved the performance. During center time they made pig paper-plate stick puppets. With our help, they performed the rap version of the nursery rhyme in the puppet theater center.

The last day of the unit was special because we went to the Green Meadows Farm on Little Neck Parkway in Queens, New York. The children saw firsthand the animals we had read about. It had rained the previous day and there was even mud for them to squish. On the ride back to school, the bus rocked to "Old MacDonald," "Bingo," and what they remembered of the rap.

When we returned to school, I again asked if they knew what a poem was. This time they were able to tell me that songs and nursery rhymes and raps are poems, that poems have words that rhyme, that you could sing a poem or clap to it. I asked which poems they liked best. They all said "funny ones" and the rap, because of the way "it moves."

During this 2-week period, the children were able to recite verses, illustrate nursery rhymes, create their own poems (with me as scribe), make a tape of a round, and play with puppets while "rapping" away. They worked collaboratively; they practiced listening and speaking, as well as prereading and writing; they learned new concepts and new vocabulary. From their enthusiastic response to everything we did, I know that they totally enjoyed themselves. And so did I.

I truly believe that children's love of poetry will grow if they are exposed pleasurably to a constant diet of poems chosen with their age and interests in mind. This was a wonderful experience for the children as well as for me, and I will increase the use of this literary form in all my thematic units.

KALIE STERN'S FIRST GRADE

I teach first grade in an inner-city school. There are 25 children in my class (13 boys and 12 girls). English is the second language of almost all the children. The nine who are receiving English as a second language (ESL) instruction are severely limited in their ability to communicate in and understand English. Many of the children are not exposed to books at home. Several are developmentally and socially delayed.

Before beginning this research project, I had to consider the children's needs, likes, dislikes, strengths, and weaknesses. Their language difficulties make the need for learning through visual means absolutely necessary. Helping them develop appropriate listening skills is also extremely important. They need opportunities to express their opinions and ideas in English.

I decided that a formal survey of what these children know about poetry would not be beneficial; instead, I surveyed by observation of their reaction to a wide range of poetry, noting their responses. I began with nursery rhymes, introducing one or two a day. Each rhyme was written on chart paper and displayed in the classroom. All of the children had turns illustrating the rhymes. I established a poetry listening center decorated with a wonderful Mother Goose poster. For the center, I made tapes of myself reciting the nursery rhymes we had read in class.

My children are absolutely fascinated by the flannel board, a board covered with flannel to which figures cut from flannel adhere. I found some cutouts of Mother Goose characters for use with a flannel board. As we recited the rhymes, children would place the appropriate picture on display.

Since my children love repetition and I know it helps them to improve their language skills, I made photocopies of each rhyme we read. With these, the children created and illustrated personal books. These were kept in their desks for use in free time or during Drop Everything and Read (DEAR) time. As I read the rhymes aloud from the charts, the children followed along in their own books.

When the children were familiar with nursery rhymes, I introduced a book called *Four and Twenty Dinosaurs* by Bernard Most (1999). He has created a very funny, entertaining book of rhymes with dinosaurs instead of regular characters. The children laughed, excited as they connected these with the rhymes they already knew of Jack and Jill, Little Miss Muffet, and others.

Kids are always full of surprises. One Friday afternoon, during playtime, I found five of them sitting at the round table in the back of the room. The children held their personal poetry books, following along as one child recited the verses. I think they were reciting from memory, not actually reading, but I didn't interrupt to find out. I think choosing to read poetry during playtime speaks for itself. There are plenty of other times to assess their reading skills.

I wanted to make poetry part of our regular routine rather than this "thing" we do every now and then. At the same time as we were immersed in Mother Goose, I added poetry to our read-aloud time after lunch. We read poems about animals, bugs, food, the seasons, the weather, friendship, the moon, even teeth. We also read most of the poems in the anthology I developed as part of the requirements for the college course. The children seemed to like the idea that these poems were my personal favorites.

One afternoon, I excitedly announced that we were going to read funny poetry. There I sat with Douglas Florian's *Bing, Bang, Boing* (1994b), anticipating the children's roaring laughter. I began with:

> Send my spinach
> Off to Spain.
> Parcel post it
> On a train.
> Mail it,
> Sail it
> On a ship.
> Just don't let it
> Touch my lip. (p. 27)

I waited. Silence. I thought, "It must be this poem; I'll try another." I read:

> If I eat more candy,
> My teeth will fall out.
> My gums will turn green
> Like the rest of my mouth.
> The dentist will drill me,
> While I scream in pain,
> A dozen long holes
> That spill into my brain.
> The stench of my breath
> Will kill birds in the air—
> But
> This candy's so good
> That I really don't care (p. 38)

Again I waited. Still quiet. Once again I thought it was the poem. So I continued with others. It was still quiet. I looked at Kathy, who had her hand up. Was she going to ask to go to the bathroom *again*?

With a serious expression on her face, she asked, "Ms. Stern, when are you going to read the funny poems?" The children were letting me know that these poems were not "it" for them. Sometimes humor is difficult for young children to understand, especially if English is not their first language. This experience taught me that I had to consider carefully the children's development—linguistic and otherwise—when choosing poems to present to them.

What they did appear to enjoy were poems that dealt with concrete things. Poems about animals and insects were among those they asked to hear again and again. They also enjoyed poems about the moon, space, and astronauts. We are working on a unit about the moon, inspired by a poem in their reader.

The onomatopoeic sounds I hear during playtime and in the yard during lunch, led me to experiment with onomatopoeia. I presented the children with a list of words: train, bird, bee, owl, wind, lion, dog, cat, pig, frog. I explained that we were going to play a game; the object was to try to make the sounds these things and creatures make. I started them off with an example: A bee goes ZZZZZZZZZ. They did well with this; they had fun and so did I.

I followed this with a reading of Taro Yashima's *Umbrella* (1977). In the book is a paragraph employing onomatopoeia to communicate the sound of the rain. After the reading, I asked the children how the rain sounded to them, listing their sounds on a chart. They included:

pit pat
click clack click clack
sh sh sh sh
tap tap tap
clink clank clink clank
P P P P P P

It rained the following day and when we discussed the weather during our morning routine, the children suggested including the sound of the rain in our class news on rainy days as we reported the weather. Of course, I agreed immediately that this was a good idea. Whenever it rains, someone reminds me that we have to include in our class news our poem that sounds like the rain. How great!

To introduce alliteration, I read *A, My Name Is Alice* by Jane Bayer (1984/1992). Then I shared some tongue twisters with the children, to their obvious enjoyment. I had alphabetized their names on chart paper; we brainstormed to find for each of them positive descriptive words beginning with the same letter as the first letter of their name. Although they needed a lot of help on this one, they were able to come up with Funny Frank, Popular Paul, Lively Levon, Smart Stanley, Merry Melissa, Artistic Adriana, and others.

I went a step further with this, beginning the process of cooperatively writing a tongue twister for each child. We used the model in the example below. With practice, the children were able to create tongue twisters like Levon's.

Lively Levon liked the lucky ladybug.
Did lively Levon like the lucky ladybug?
If lively Levon liked the lucky ladybug,
Where is the lucky ladybug that lovable Levon liked?

When I started this ongoing poetry project, I didn't know where or how to begin. I felt that the poetic possibilities with these children were so limited. Soon I realized that poetry could be experienced and enjoyed if presented in a context to which they could relate. We are learning a great deal together. My observations of the children reveal a growing enjoyment and developing understanding of poetry, verse, and unusual uses of language.

Poetic language comes naturally to the children. They use poetic devices like rhythm and alliteration in their daily speech. At playtime, I hear them chanting taunts or calling out alliterative comments to each other. I tried to use this as a place to begin more formal work with poetry. The children are learning that poetry is good reading material that they can handle because it is repetitive, rhythmic, and usually short. They are learning about poetry by experiencing it rather than trying to define or describe it.

KERRY FARRELL'S SECOND GRADE

I believe my not teaching poetry previously in my classroom is partly because my own early teachers never sparked an interest in it and partly due to the inadequacy I felt in high school poetry classes. There I felt insecure and confused, unable to see the underlying messages teachers claimed were in the poems we studied. Poetry study meant regurgitating the teachers' ideas to pass tests. As a result, I shied away from teaching poetry in my own classroom.

As a challenge to me and my students, I decided to give poetry a chance. It was the least we could do. I began by asking the children to

> "Comparisons have to be fresh in order to have the best effect: if you write 'red as a rose,' few readers will see a rose, fewer still will smell one. . . ." Red as a rose" is so familiar that a reader is most likely to take in the whole phrase at once, to accept it automatically, and not to see or feel anything (Kenneth Koch, 1998, p. 53).

recall their encounters with poetry. These recollections were meager. One had written a short rhyming poem in first grade to earn a grade. Several expressed apprehension about being asked to write poetry. They couldn't offer examples of reading a poem on their own or even listening to a poem read aloud. Although many admitted familiarity with Mother Goose rhymes, they never saw these as poetry. Their book reviews included no poetry books.

My first step in a poetry project with these children was to become familiar myself with all types of poetry books containing poems with appeal for second graders. I knew I had my work cut out for me. I combed anthologies to find poems on topics I thought my children would enjoy, such as the seasons, sports, holidays, birthdays, friendship, and family. I found many of these listed in one of our textbooks, *Essentials of Children's Literature: A Critical Handbook of Children's Literature* (Tomlinson & Lynch-Brown, 1993). A search of book sites on the Internet was helpful (amazon .com, barnesandnoble.com, and scholastic.com).

Besides selecting poems on topics of interest to my children, I chose those with vocabulary that was for the most part within their reach and began to read them aloud. Unfamiliar words, once identified and defined, were added to our word wall, a posting of words we have learned. I chose short poems for reading aloud more than once. I found poems in a variety of forms. The children enjoyed most the ones that rhymed and were humorous. I took Dr. Sloan's (1991) advice: "Poems chosen for children should speak to them at their level of understanding, but they ought also to stretch minds and imaginations with fresh insights, novel ways of seeing the world, and unusual but apt ways with words" (p. 99). I brought in a wide selection of poetry books to set up a poetry center so the children could browse during DEAR (Drop Everything and Read) time.

I read poems aloud every minute I could. I chose the poems to fit the activity we were doing and what we were experiencing: the news my students shared, the weather, the holiday around the corner, and so on. Warm days invited poems from *Lemonade Sun and Other Summer Poems* (Dotlich, 2001). *The Grapes of Math: Mind Stretching Math Riddles* (Tang, 2001) was a good accompaniment to solving math problems.

Both students and I were surprised that we were able to find poems to fit into any situation of our day. I was relieved to discover this; I wanted to use plenty of poetry but I also was required to stay within the curriculum. Soon the children brought in poems to share aloud with the class. I encouraged them to read in pairs as well. Their enjoyment of the wonders of poetry was obvious. I saw the poems come to life in the eyes, ears, and hearts of my children.

Some tried to repeat the rhymes they heard. They begged to hear favorites read again. They read poems to one another every chance they got, sometimes bringing books outdoors during lunch break. Parents helping out at lunch were impressed that second graders would rather giggle over the poems they were reading than run around the playground. I received compliments from parents and the principal, who noticed a changed mood among my students. They were living one of my goals for them: to learn and have fun at the same time. I realized that poetry could help me teach the curriculum, not subtract time from it.

Young children need to move; sitting quietly is a chore. With poetry, they could clap the beat, sway, or move to it. I encouraged them to interpret the movements of animals described in poems. At times the room became noisy but the noise meant the children were involved. Now that I knew something of the power of poetry to interest children in words, I began to use a book of choral readings. I copied the poems, assigned parts, held practices, and watched these beginning readers hone their reading skills while they had a good time.

We responded to the poems through discussion. I avoided asking the children to tell me what the poems meant. Instead, I invited them to comment about the poems while I recorded their responses. To my surprise, they did respond, connecting the poems to their everyday lives and their memories. They commented on language that interested or confused them. When we had dozens and dozens of poetry experiences behind us, I felt my students were able to put their thoughts and feelings into written words. We began to write poetry.

We started with a group poem. I asked the music teacher for a simple melody for the keyboard. The children, choosing summer as their theme, chanted lines to the melody, among them, "Summer is cool" and "You can swim in the pool," until we had contributions from nearly everyone. We explored our five senses and put our experiences into words. I used Kenneth Koch's (1970) format, "I used to be . . . /But now I am . . ." to prime writing. We used many techniques I gleaned from teachers' resources.

A favorite was what the children called the Word Bowl. I collected all the reading words studied since September in a large plastic bowl. From it, I picked 10 words at random and wrote them on the board. In pairs students worked to create interesting variations on these groups of words. In subsequent writing workshops, individuals or groups chose words and created groupings with them. Where necessary, they could add words or exchange them. They were to avoid creating sentences and encouraged to make associative connections among words. They were encouraged to arrange and paste their words on drawing paper, even to include them within a picture. This activity, while perhaps not producing timeless poetry, produces keen interest in words.

I have made a beginning in poetry with my students. I see that what they and I have done together has caused a new spark in us, a new interest in reading and writing words. I wasn't reading poetry myself or presenting it to my class until I undertook this assignment for my college class. What an exciting adventure it has become!

JOAN POPPER-KANE'S THIRD GRADE

I conducted this study in my third-grade classroom at St. Joseph School in Astoria, New York. The students are mostly White English-speaking children of working-class parents. Most of the children read at or above grade level. I used the sustained silent reading time and part of the afternoon each day for this study. Each session was 45–60 minutes long. Previously, I had hardly ever read poetry to my class, mainly because I had had such a bad experience in high school with poetry that I didn't particularly care for it. I read the poems in the basal reader, but I never went beyond that. One of the reasons I took this poetry course was to learn more about poetry for children. I knew that my class was missing out, but I was unaware of what was out there in terms of poetry for children.

As a result of my survey, I found that most of my class did like poetry but did not read it very often and never wrote it. I decided to inundate them with the work of poets we'd heard about in the college class; eventually, I wanted them to try to write some poems of their own.

From the public school and Queens College libraries, I borrowed as many poetry books as I could carry. It took me 2 days to get them all to school, where I displayed them along the chalkboard and on a table. The children were very curious about this large collection of books.

The first day of our study, each child made and decorated a poetry journal. I asked if anyone knew a poem. Nobody answered. I wanted them to discover that they knew a lot of poems; they just didn't realize this. I began to read them various nursery rhymes, including "Little Miss Muffet," "Jack and Jill," and "Old King Cole." Before long, the children were reciting with me and then calling out for others they knew. Someone said, "What about 'Humpty Dumpty'?" We recited it together. For more than 20 minutes we read and recited, laughing together.

Then we took time for the children to write in their journals. The responses were almost all positive. Ashley wrote, "I was surprised that a song like 'This Old Man' is a poem: "I never knew I knew so many poems." "I thought that nursery rhymes were for little kids," Nicole wrote. "I didn't know they are poems; I already know a lot of them." I also wrote in my journal at this time. After each child wrote a response to our first session, he or she selected a poetry book to browse through. We were off to a good start.

In session two, we jumped right into poetry. In collections of poems by Kali Dakos, Jack Prelutsky, and David Harrison, I found good poems about school and read them to the class. I had to read Prelutsky's (1984) "Homework O Homework" (p. 54) three times; by the third time, the children were reciting it. They wanted their own copies of the poem and I made copies for them. In her journal that day Kathryn said, "Today I loved 'Homework O Homework.' I never even knew that I liked poetry, but I do."

In the third session, I shared longer poems, some of them serious, asking the children to pick one poem and write a response to it in their journals. "'Twas the Night Before Christmas" (Moore, 1823/1999) elicited the strongest response. Kaitlin wrote that it made her feel "nice and warm inside."

In session four, my purpose was to introduce the students to some of the outstanding authors who write verse for children. I gave a few book talks on some of the books I had brought into the classroom. I read many selections from Douglas Florian's *Beast Feast* (1994a) and *Bing, Bang, Boing* (1994b). I chose several from Jack Prelutsky's *Something Big Has Been Here* (1990) and *New Kid on the Block* (1984). I read "Celery," "The Canary," and "The People Upstairs" by Ogden Nash (1980). The children loved these so much that they asked for more. I read every poem I could find by Ogden Nash. They couldn't get enough of him; everyone was all bent over laughing. After the reading, each child picked a book to browse in. Many of them found a partner and read to one another. Soon they were copying favorite poems into their journals, transforming the journals into personal anthologies.

In sessions five and six, I began by reading poems by Langston Hughes. The children liked them, but they liked the humorous poems better. After I read aloud, the children again chose books from the collection and, in groups of two or three, sat looking through them, from time to time reading aloud to one another. The classroom buzzed with laughter. They continued copying their favorites into their journals. Among the most popular books were *Beast Feast, Something Big Has Been Here,* and *Sing a Song of Popcorn* (de Regniers, 1988).

In the second phase of my poetry unit, I set up a poetry writing workshop. Since everyone in my class had answered False to the statement "I am a poet" on the initial survey, I decided that this was an area that needed attention. I would not have attempted this had I not read *For the Good of the Earth and the Sun* by Georgia Heard (1989). I followed her suggestions, especially what she said about the importance of conferencing and the best way to go about it.

I began the writing workshop with the "terse verse" that Bruce McMillan uses in several of his books. I knew that not only would the children have fun with this simple two-word form but also it would build confidence. I wrote several examples and drew pictures to accompany them. With all the children sitting on mats around the chart, I unveiled my work. They laughed hysterically over my drawings and sayings, among them Tall Paul, Whale Tale, and Creature Feature.

Together we brainstormed some ideas for terse verse. There was a temptation to sacrifice sense to make a rhyme, any rhyme. When this happened, I asked, "How would you draw that?" Having to illustrate their terse verses kept them focused on making sense. After we created some together, the children each wrote their own. When these were illustrated, I arranged them in the hallway under a banner that read "Poetry Is Words That Sing," borrowing the title of a film we saw in the college class. The display included Easter Beaster (picture of a rabbit), Purple Gerbil, Bird Nerd (drawing of an owl), and Mountain Fountain (waterfall).

In later sessions, we worked on rhyming couplets and on making a poem with several related couplets. (Many of the children just enjoyed the *sound* of the words "rhyming couplets.") I read examples of poems written in couplets, copying some on chart paper so the children could see how the form looked as they listened. At first, we worked together to brainstorm and create. Then the children wrote independently, although they shared ideas and helped one another. I think they were very successful in their poetry writing. Certainly they were absorbed in their work.

I conferenced regularly with the children. They needed help with spacing as well as beginning and ending the lines. In the conferences, I asked the children to read the poem aloud twice: the first time just to hear it; the second time to notice where their voice paused. The students then rewrote their poems as they wanted them read. This method, besides putting the students in control of their poetry, was effective in improving sense and form.

We experimented with putting several couplets together to make a longer poem, a common poetic form, as the children discovered. Here is Christopher's:

Alien, Alien, take me away,
Out of this galaxy called Milky Way;
Take me to your planet,
Show me your leader, Titanic;
Show me your weapons made of silver
And how to destroy a monster killer.

Another form we tried to write was haiku, partly because it fit perfectly into our unit on Japan. I asked the children to bring in a magazine picture of something in nature. I copied and illustrated on chart paper many haiku from *The Haiku Anthology* (Van den Huevel, 2000). I explained the haiku form. From the examples I read, the children concluded that haiku were about nature and understood the purpose of bringing to class nature pictures. Each child looked at his or her picture and described it. With help from me and one another, they rearranged the words to fit the haiku pattern. I was very pleasantly surprised at the results. Some of the boys preferred to write about sports, inventing a totally new form of haiku.

A moon—bright as light—
Moon rises in the sky,
And creatures come out.—Ryan

Shaquille O'Neil shoots
In the cool, fanned stadium;
The net and ball meet.—Christopher

The week before Mother's Day, the children were making flowers and cards for their mothers. A group suggested that it would be cool to write a poem for the occasion. All 29 children abandoned their coloring and crafts to write poetry. What an amazing sight! I was so proud. Some of the children wrote acrostics, some tried haiku, and some tried free verse, which we hadn't studied formally but they had picked up from their reading. Daniel wrote:

Mom, you're full of love;
Good things happen all around you.
When I look at you I see hearts in your eyes;
You get prettier every day

Because you are my mom;
You're always there when I need you.
Don't ever change.

I never would have guessed that my poetry unit could be so successful. I didn't have to formally resurvey the class to see whether the unit was
a success in changing attitudes and building knowledge about poetry. The
enthusiasm and obvious interest in reading and writing poetry speak for
themselves. I know that I have changed the lives of 29 third graders and
changed my own life, too.

BEATRICE LASKI'S FOURTH GRADE

Designing a poetry study with fourth graders is a challenge, because
fourth graders are the target of the English language arts tests. Most prin-
cipals insist on concentrating on test materials. The new standards do require, however, that children be introduced to various genres, including
poetry. If teachers are clever and creative, they can include poetry, an important contributor to literacy development, in the curriculum.

I began with a survey to determine what the children knew about poetry and their attitude toward it. Asked to define poetry, they said it was
"the expression of personal feelings," "writing that rhymes," "language
talking about love, flowers, yourself, and friendship." The survey indicated
that the children did not read poetry on their own; only two could name a
poet or offer the titles of poems they knew. A few had written haiku in
previous classes.

The descriptive language, the imagery of poetry that creates sensory
impressions for the reader, was my first emphasis in choosing poems to
read aloud. As the children listened to poems by Shel Silverstein (1974,
1981) and Avis Harley (2000), they identified the descriptive words that
created vivid sensory images. I read examples of metaphoric poems from
Poem-Making (Livingston, 1991), among them Eve Merriam's "From the
Japanese" and "Metaphor," and Valerie Worth's "Sun."

We tried an exercise: I asked the students what images come to mind
when they think of the color red, prompting them by asking what red looks
like, feels like, sounds like, and smells like. I recorded their responses,
writing them with line breaks.

Red is tomatoes
Growing in grandma's garden;
A rose freshly picked;

"What I usually find with younger writers is that they write so generally, write so widely that they don't communicate to the reader. What we like to hear are the really intimate details of all our lives" (Gary Soto in Copeland, 1993/1994, Vol. I, p. 92).

Sunburn after a day at Rockaway Beach;
Catsup on hot fries;
A fire truck racing down an alley.

As we read poems, the students discovered how they were put together. Since the children loved rhyme, I chose some poems for them that featured rhyming couplets, many of them from *The Random House Book of Poetry for Children* (Prelutsky, 1983a). While the children enjoyed hearing and reading couplets, at first they had difficulty writing them well. The tendency was to toss in any word that rhymed, never mind the sense. We talked about rearranging lines to find meaningful rhymes. In the process we learned that it is not so easy to create good rhyming couplets. When we had mastered the art to some extent, we went on to quatrains, two couplets in a stanza. With these, we found it was good to have a story to tell. The students also found that reading their work aloud was helpful in locating poor rhymes and rhythm; they each learned that it was easier to revise their classmates' work than their own.

Taking the advice of Paul Janeczko (2000), we tried acrostics. We examined variations of the form most familiar: words and phrases beginning in turn with the letters of the poem's subject. We also found acrostics where the subject is spelled out in the middle or at the end of the lines. Our own acrostic celebrated the principal, Ms. Winfree, and we presented it to her at her retirement party.

Wonderful principal
Is always improving our school;
Never will be forgotten,
Forever in control,
Respecting of all differences,
Encourages all children to do their best.
Everyone's friend.

Next the children wrote acrostics that described themselves, striving for vivid images to round out facts (or fictions) about themselves.

A favorite exercise for the students was one that truly piqued their interest in words. I began by showing them the one-word poem by Robert Carola, STOWAWAY (Janeczko, 2001, p. 9). Immediately the students grasped the idea of arranging words to create dramatic effect. These poems catch the eye by the way they are arranged on the page. I wrote Jump and Run on the board, asking the students to rewrite the words in a way that would illustrate their meanings. Jump became an inverted V with JU going up the page and MP coming down the page. Run acquired feet on its letters. Vivid word pictures were created with words of their own choosing: waterfall, flip, smile, and twister.

The book of shape poems, *Doodle Dandies* (Lewis, 1998a), was the inspiration for the more complicated shape poems we tried next. Before working individually to present shape poems on footballs, pencils, and books, we worked together with the word *sun*. I asked for their words to describe the sun: how the sun makes them feel, what things they associate with the sun. All these responses were recorded. Then we discussed what shape our poem should take. The students chose the style where the shape of the image is created with words and phrases, filling in the shape rather than outlining it.

We experimented with alliteration, beginning, amid laughter, to trip over the tongue twisters we tried to recite. Our own alliterative creations included: "Crazy conversations could create confusion," "Dave drove dangerously," "Jaleel juggles joyfully." The children (and I) created alliterative statements about ourselves, using our names.

Among our other experiences and adventures with words was attempting to correctly rearrange the cut-up lines of a short unrhymed poem. This exercise helped the children to become aware of line breaks, among other things.

Another form we tried was the cinquain, a great way to introduce nonrhyming poetry because rhyme is seldom used. The cinquain's five-line form follows a set pattern of syllables: 2, 4, 6, 8, 2. I didn't tell the children this; they told me. We wrote a collaborative poem about babies before the children tried cinquains of their own. We listed words or phrases describing babies, actions related to them, how we feel about them, and what we associate with them. Here is the poem:

Babies:
Powdery smells,
Energetic at night,
Cause of sleepless nights for others,
But sweet.

I counted my work with the children on poetry a success. The children now enjoyed listening to poetry. They sought out poetry books in the library. They shared poems with friends and family. Where they once knew no names of poets, they now had favorites among the many poets they had been introduced to. They had all tried writing poetry in a variety of forms. Surveys taken at the end of our study confirmed that all involved had new and positive perceptions about this exciting genre.

REGINA FURNARI'S FIFTH GRADE

The subjects of this study were 10 boys and 12 girls in my fifth-grade class at Our Lady of the Blessed Sacrament School in Bayside, Queens, New York. Their cultural backgrounds included Caucasian, Hispanic, and Asian. This sample, heterogeneously grouped, had a wide range of reading and writing abilities. My first step was to find out their views about poetry. An informal survey through class discussion revealed that all the girls and only one boy claimed to like poetry. Reasons for not liking it included: "It's boring" and "It doesn't make sense." I was determined to prove to these children that poetry can be fun.

I began by literally immersing the students in poetry. I hung poems by various authors around the classroom: on the chalkboard, next to the fish bowl, in the writing center and the social studies and math centers. On my classroom door, I hung a copy of Shel Silverstein's (1974) "Invitation," which invites dreamers, wishers, liars (that is to say, poets) to come in.

Knowing that riddles, which describe things in terms of other related or even unrelated things, are the very essence of poetry, my brain teaser board in the classroom featured a different riddle each day. Many different riddle poems, such as "The Man from St. Ives," were used. I found the students running into the classroom each morning to read and solve each new riddle. Soon they were bringing in riddles themselves for their classmates to solve.

In addition to this daily exposure to riddles, I read a poem to the class every day after lunch, sharing my enthusiasm for favorite selections by A. A. Milne, Eve Merriam, X. J. Kennedy, Gary Soto, Janet Wong, and others in our classroom library of poetry. After a few days, the students asked to read aloud *their* favorites. This varied experience emphasized that everyone has different preferences. Some like a poem for its content; others especially appreciate the way it sounds; and some just like the way it looks on the page.

Well into our sharing sessions, I began a series of more formal workshops in reading and writing poetry. The first workshop was called Rhym-

> [On writing poetry] "See the world and smell the world and wonder about the world. Experience the beauty in everything. And then if you can share your feelings with someone else, that will be an added delight" (Aileen Fisher in Copeland, 1993/1994, Vol. I, p. 33).

ing Slogans. At first, I made no mention of "poetry." Instead, I mentioned that our health project display was drab and perhaps needed the excitement of a slogan. Previously, the health classes had constructed cigarette boxes with product names and statements to discourage smoking. Now I put them to work finding effective slogans in magazines. We examined the best ones, studying the techniques that made them stand out: word play, alliteration, rhyme.

Then the children wrote original slogans with an antismoking theme. They came up with more than 20, including "If you smoke, you're a joke," "If you start smoking, you must be joking," and "If you smoke, you're sure to croak." At the end of the session, the students were energized, interested, and pleased with their success. This included those who said they didn't like poetry!

In introducing terse verse, a form that artist-photographer Bruce McMillan uses to great effect, I explained that a poem doesn't have to be long. It can be as short as two rhyming words. I read Bruce McMillan's *One Sun* (1990), which amused them, although they thought—and rightly—that they were too old for this simple book. I agreed, but I wanted them to practice terse verse, so I suggested that they write some and publish them for use in the primary grades. We brainstormed, collaboratively came up with a list of terse verse, then wrote independently. The best of the two-word rhymes were illustrated and collected as *The Big Book of Terse Verse*. The book was circulated to all the first and second grades in the school. My students were excited by their rave reviews.

To begin a session on couplets, we read Maya Angelou's *Life Doesn't Frighten Me* (1978/1993). We examined the form together and discussed the content. With partners, the children talked about things that frighten them. Then they turned their list of fears into a triplet, with the third a repeating line: "Life doesn't frighten me at all." Some wrote couplets on this theme, and others extended their couplets into quatrains. We "grew" the poem together, collecting quatrains and couplets on chart paper. Here is part of it:

It doesn't bother me when I hit a wall,
Or someone hits me with a ball;

I don't cry and run through the hall,
I just pick myself up from where I fall;
Life doesn't frighten me at all.

In another lesson, I wanted to make the point that poems and verse can be found everywhere. The children were skeptical; they insisted that outside of school this was certainly not true. Those who claimed not to like poetry protested the loudest. They were amazed when I recited the lyrics of a rock ballad familiar to them and were astonished to discover that it was in the form of a quatrain.

Students worked in pairs or individually to try their hand at writing quatrains on any subject that interested them. I wrote, sharing my work and getting their suggestions on improving it. They noticed that, for my college class, I was working on a volume of original verse. They decided to make a class book of their creations. No one was forced to contribute, but most did.

Our workshop on limerick writing was one the students had looked forward to. They had some experience with limericks and were prepared to laugh as I read aloud examples. To get them to note the form, I read two aloud. One had the correct form; the other did not. I concentrated on sound. The class was able to identify the correct form because it "sounded right." I sang for them and we snapped our fingers to reinforce the correct rhythm.

Again they worked in pairs or individually, this time to create limericks. We used many revision techniques during my conferences with the students. In some cases, the work was set aside for another day. Finally, several were completed in this challenging form and included in the class anthology. Here is one example by Elizabeth:

There once was a captain named Kirk,
I thought he was really a jerk.
He went out into space,
Fell flat on his face,
And that was the end of his work.

Cinquain writing was the workshop I most looked forward to. I had a good experience writing my own cinquain during the semester and I couldn't wait to share my enthusiasm with the students. I copied David McCord's (1970) poem "Cinquain" on a transparency for the overhead projector and shared it with the class. They protested, "That's not a poem; it doesn't rhyme!" I read some of my cinquains to them, explaining that not all poems have to rhyme. I gave them more examples; together we discussed the characteristics of the form as they discovered them.

Eventually they were able to count the syllables correctly by speaking them aloud and tapping with fingers. They were able to employ run-on lines to create the genuine cinquains that David McCord's (1970) examples—the one on the left— taught them to write.

Do you	Do you
Care for crickets?	Care for apples?
I love their summer sound	I love their smooth round cheeks.
Late fall I like one in a house	And how with each bite juice spurts in
Chirping. (p. 96)	my mouth.

I used Georgia Heard's (1989) re-visioning technique, which involves closing your eyes, picturing something you especially like, seeing it in detail, and then describing it. I circulated to help as the students experimented with writing cinquain. Some were openly opposed to the idea of nonrhyming poetry, to the extent of writing cinquains about how much they hated the form. But by the end of the session, almost all of the students had produced a smooth cinquain, true to form.

During this 8-week concentration on poetry, my class explored poetry in many ways. Opportunities to share their favorites allowed them to discover that they *had* favorites; eagerness to share overcame fears of reading aloud to others. They learned to appreciate other poems besides the humorous ones they loved. They discovered to their amazement just how many types of poems are out there for their enjoyment.

In our many writing workshops, students learned that writing is a process and not always a simple one. Even the best of poets seldom sit down and immediately produce a publishable poem. Time, patience, hard work, and helpful advice from others are all part of the process. During and after the poetry unit, students were eager to share their work with others and get feedback on language, style, and form.

When I conducted the postunit survey on attitudes toward poetry, 13 of the 22 students said they had really enjoyed the unit. Six told me that they enjoyed poetry more than before. This information and the work they produced convince me that this was a successful project.

ELIZABETH SCHNEIDER'S SIXTH GRADE

The 26 students in my reading group are considered to be on the lowest level across sixth grade. Fifty-eight percent test below grade level in reading; 15% receive resource room services; 19% are in ESL programs.

"Every poem is music—a determined, persuasive, reliable, enthusiastic, and crafted music" (Mary Oliver, 1998, p. ix).

Since for the most part these students have struggled all their school lives with literacy, many of them fear and dislike reading and writing. My goal was to show them that reading and literacy development in general can be enjoyable and fun. I spent a lot of time researching the perfect book to help me achieve this goal. I finally settled on *Out of the Dust*, the Newbery Award winner by Karen Hesse (1998).

This excellent book combines two genres: historical fiction and poetry. Careful research allowed Hesse to recreate vividly the dust storms of the Depression of the 1930s in the western United States. At the same time the author tells, in a series of free verse poems, a compelling story of Billie Jo, a plucky teenage girl who copes with tragedy and loss in a harsh environment from which there seems to be no escape.

I introduced the book by reading aloud the first poems (chapters). For each poem, the students kept a log with two columns, one for the historical understandings they gained from the book and one for language or images that interested, pleased, or baffled them. The logs were the basis for prompts to guide our group discussion of the poems. The students found the verse format, with its flowing prose and shorter lines, easier to read on their own than the traditional novel form.

My students soon learned how rich were the images in *Out of the Dust*. We discussed how the author used words to help the reader visualize or experience a strong emotion. In an exercise that worked well, I had the children recast an image in the their own words and create an illustration for it. Hesse describes Billie Jo's father as "stubborn as sod"; a student called him "as inflexible as dry grass." I felt that this exercise made poetry more accessible to the students. They needn't be afraid that they would be wrong as they created images of their own. The model was there; the original image served as a security blanket.

Students also responded to this book with free verse poems and letters to and from different characters in the book. The best free verse came out of situations involving strong emotions, such as the death of Billie Jo's mother. To bolster the students' attempts to write free verse, we read and attempted to write cinquain. One student response to the book was a poem in the shape of a square, with words about Billie Jo's situation arranged around the square, illustrative of the girl's entrapment in a cheerless place and an unhappy situation.

Our in-depth study of a novel in verse had another aspect. We had the opportunity during our study to work with a poet and mime artist. Under his guidance the children interpreted and enacted scenes from the novel. Response to the poems of the book through movement and art seemed to have a highly positive effect on my students, keeping their interest, helping them to focus, and facilitating their writing. Poet Eve Merriam advises young poets not to intellectualize, but to respond to words with movement: "Use your whole body as you write. It might even help sometimes to stand up and move with your words" (Sloan, 1991, p. 95).

For these nonbookish students who are not particularly interested in words, the concept of a novel told in verse was intriguing. One parent reported that she had never known her son to be so interested in schoolwork. Students asked if there was a sequel to *Out of the Dust*. There isn't, but *Witness* is another historical fiction by Karen Hesse (2001) in free verse. Among other excellent stories in verse for this age group are Mel Glenn's mystery, *Who Killed Mr. Chippendale?* (1996), and Virginia Euwer Wolf's *True Believer* (2001).

DIANE PECK'S SEVENTH AND EIGHTH GRADES

My class of seventh and eighth graders in a private school take English together. A fairly large quantity of good poetry from a variety of authors is studied, using a comprehensive literature anthology that includes poetry and prose. The stated goal of our literature work in junior high is the appreciation of fine literature. These students have all attended private schools for most of their educational lives. Throughout their years in school, poetry has been included as part of the curriculum, although not to the extent it is in junior high. Most of the poetry studied is classical: "Paul Revere's Ride," "The Pied Piper of Hamelin," selections from Lewis Carroll, and the like. Supplementation is at the discretion of the classroom teacher.

I began by administering a survey to the class to assess their interest in and knowledge of poetry. The students' responses indicated a moderately positive attitude toward poetry, with the average response to most questions slightly above neutral. All except one member of the class reported owning at least one volume of poetry. All said that they never take out poetry books from the library and that they mostly read and write poetry only in school. Asked about their familiarity with various forms such as limerick, nursery rhyme, cinquain, haiku, free verse, acrostic, quatrain, lyric, narrative, shape poem, and couplet, the students claimed to be familiar with an average of six forms and to have written at least four.

Most students did not have a favorite poet. Asked to name a poet, 90% did, naming "adult" poets such as Whitman, Poe, Longfellow, Homer, Horace, and Sandburg.

I used the information from the survey to plan a poetry unit for the class. One goal of the project was to expose these students to more "youthful" poetry before they entered high school. I hoped to show them that poetry could be a lighthearted, joyful experience, as well as a cultural benefit. It seemed to me that there was an educational lapse here. We had worked diligently to introduce fine literature into our students' lives, but we seemed to have omitted material with the potential for fostering a higher level of interest in this literature. I believe that there is a place for both approaches. It was time to have some fun.

I decided to begin with a basic verse form: the couplet. Since the survey indicated that the students preferred poetry that rhymed, I considered it wise to start by supporting this preference. The first item I presented was *Old Black Fly* by Jim Aylesworth (1998). This colorful picture book is written entirely in extremely ridiculous couplets, accompanied by outrageous illustrations. Although obviously written with a younger audience in mind, the sly sense of humor in the material appealed to older youngsters.

After we read it and laughed, we discussed the various poetic forms and conventions Aylesworth had used. Working inductively, they noted alliteration, repetition, and rhyme, and were introduced to assonance. They saw that the rhyme scheme was *aabb* and learned that the term for two lines that rhyme is "couplet."

The next day we read together David McCord's (1962) poem "Write Me a Verse." In it Professor Brown instructs his students on various forms of poetry, beginning with the couplet. McCord uses the poem to introduce the concept of the couplet's meter as well as its rhyme scheme. Students searched anthologies for poems written in rhyming couplets. They shared their findings with the class. Next they wrote couplets themselves, independently or with a partner, on subjects they chose. Their best efforts went into their poetry folders.

Professor Brown also discusses limericks. We read the appropriate portions of McCord's poem, but I did not feel that this was successful. McCord seemed to get away from the clever limerick into a more involved, "literate" limerick. The students had trouble discovering the form from his examples. I decided to present, by reading aloud, a large selection of more standard limericks from various collections. The students worked in groups, immersed in limericks, reading to themselves and one another.

After they had heard many examples and examined the form, discovering its characteristics, the students tried writing their own limericks. Many of the students experienced difficulty with this form. In those cases, they filed their attempts in their folders, deciding to revisit and rework them another time. Vicki wrote about Vicki with this result:

> There once was a girl named Vicki,
> She was extremely picky.
> When it came to clothes,
> How well she knows
> That picking out clothes can be tricky.

Having had success with choral readings and readers' theater presentations of poetry, I decided to use Paul Fleischman's *Joyful Noise* (1988) with the class. The book is a collection of poems for two voices. The children enjoyed preparing and performing these readings in pairs. When they asked for more, I brought out *I Am Phoenix* (Fleischman, 1985), a similar collection. Pairs of readers were remixed for this second book, again with excellent performance results. We would have kept going if we'd had more material.

One afternoon was spent creating "found" poetry from magazines brought in by the students. To create this form, students find words and phrases that for them relate in some way, snip them out of the magazine or newspaper, and make a "poetic" arrangement of them on a blank page. They produced a wide variety of unusual and clever themes, which they shared aloud and then posted in our room for a colorful display. Visitors check out this display since it is both eye-catching and quick to read. Everyone enjoyed this activity, but we worried that it was too lightweight and easy to do. None of us is too sure that this form is "really" poetry. The whole issue of what poetry is or is not is discussed by Dr. Sloan in "But Is It Poetry?" (2001). She maintains that poetry occurs on a broad spectrum, all the way from nonliterary jingles to "serious" poetry widely acknowledged as literary. To develop discrimination in poetry, readers need to experience it in all its forms, from one end of the spectrum to the other.

Studying narrative poetry was a good way to look at both classic story poems like Alfred Noyes's "The Highwayman" (1991) and modern tales of Shel Silverstein and others. The work of poets like Ogden Nash shows that story poems can be humorous. We noted how these stories often are told in quatrains, which are arrangements of two couplets. The students were encouraged to try writing a story poem of their own, perhaps using a Bible story or fairy tale as the basis for their retelling. This work is still in progress, because it is a project that requires plenty of time. As Natasha put it:

Poetry requires a lot of time,
When you are thinking of words that rhyme.
You can think, wonder, ponder, and stare,
But when you look back, there's still nothing there.
Sometimes you think of a sentence that's great,
But when you reread it, it's a sentence you hate!

Of all my efforts to "lighten up" poetry for my students, my favorite activity was the poetry wallow. On Friday afternoon, dressed in our gym clothes, we pushed back our desks. Then we got down on the floor with a large pile of brand-new poetry books by all the authors these students had missed in earlier grades: Karla Kuskin, Valerie Worth, Myra Cohn Livingston, Judith Viorst, Aileen Fisher, Barbara Esbensen, Alice Schertle, and many others. As we wallowed around and sampled the poems, there was only one requirement: Students had to read at least two poems from a book before putting it down. They were encouraged to share the wealth by reading to one another. Most seemed to enjoy the selections; all were productively engaged in the exercise. This activity had the added virtue of being eyed jealously by other classes. We looked as though we were having fun!

At the conclusion of the unit, the students took the survey of attitudes and knowledge again. Most telling were the comments elicited when the students were asked to tell if and how their attitude toward poetry had changed over the course of the unit. Here are a few of the comments: "I learned that poetry doesn't always have to be boring." "Poetry can be dumb, and silly, and FUN!" "I think more highly of poetry than I used to."

These types of comments encouraged me to believe that I had achieved one of my goals: to develop a more positive view of poetry by introducing the youthful, amusing types of poetry that my students were not used to hearing and reading. I am also encouraged to continue using this wider range of poetry. Now that I know more about "children's" poets with special appeal for this age group, I want my students to meet them. They can enrich the students' lives.

CONCLUSION

Clearly, these examples of classroom practice, representative of scores more success stories, indicate that where there is thoughtful teaching and preparation to ensure enjoyable engagement with poetry and verse, children respond with delight. Unfortunately, there is relatively little research on the effect of poetry to develop a positive attitude toward literacy or to improve skill in reading or writing. McClure, Harrison, and Reed (1990) tell of a year in a classroom where poetry was set at the center of the curriculum. The results were highly positive in the development of both attitudes and skills. More such research surely would move poetry from the periphery to the forefront of the curriculum in literacy development. This development results always from an interest in written words, and these accounts confirm that poetry and verse arouse interest. Without this interest, there will be, among young students, little voluntary reading of words and minimal attempt to write them.

CHAPTER 5

Words of Wisdom:
"It's Music Without the Band"

Not all students in my poetry class are currently teaching. Lacking a class-room, they must find subjects for the action research projects described in the previous chapter. Often the nonteaching students press their own or borrowed children into the service of the project, with gratifying results. Selected accounts of their experiences are included here to guide parents interested in designing a shared poetry experience with their child.

POETRY PROJECTS OUTSIDE THE CLASSROOM

Maryann and Thomas Seubert

My 7-year-old son, Thomas, was enthusiastic about helping me with my homework. Questioning him, I discovered that he enjoyed reading in a variety of literary genres, especially biographies "about baseball players and people in history like Abraham Lincoln." Asked about poetry, he said it was "all right" but he didn't know much about it. We agreed to work on poetry together.

To begin, I read aloud from *The Nonsense Poems of Edward Lear* (1991). Then we tried A. A. Milne (1924). He loved the poems about Pooh and the talking cow in "The King's Breakfast." Next we read from *A Jar of Tiny Stars* (Cullinan, 1995). The imagery of a pencil having rooms in "Pencils" by Barbara Esbensen intrigued Thomas, and the rhythm of Eve Merriam's "Skip Rope Rhyme" had him pretending to jump rope.

Thomas enjoyed Karla Kuskin's "Lewis Has a Trumpet" (Cullinan, 1996) so much that he began looking for more poems by this poet. He was collecting for a personal anthology, browsing through the 25 different types of anthologies I had made available. I asked him to practice reading his selections for later reading aloud to me. (Dr. Sloan insists that no one should read "cold"; practice must precede oral reading.)

I also wanted him to explain the reasons for his choices. Most were on subjects of interest; "Sick Days" by Mary Ann Hoberman (1991) struck a personal chord. "I don't like being sick," said Thomas, "but it's fun sometimes because you take special care of me like the mother in the poem."

In coaching Thomas's reading aloud, I used questions from *Three Voices: An Invitation to Poetry Across the Curriculum* (Cullinan, Scala, & Schroder, 1995): Where did we read slowly? Quickly? Loudly? Softly? Where did we stop or pause? Why? (p. 16). I noticed how Thomas spontaneously had memorized lines and phrases of poems, often repeating them in conversation.

Learning is made meaningful through making connections, in this case among literary and nonliterary experiences (Sloan, 1991). I followed through on this idea with Thomas. After reading an article on bats in *National Geographic World*, we read poems about bats; at World Series time, we concentrated on baseball poems.

An encounter with Jack Prelutsky's (1996) spiral-shaped poem, "A Dizzy Little Duzzle" (p. 137), began an interest in shape poems, especially those found in *A Poke in the I* (Janeczko, 2001) and *Seeing Things* (Froman, 1974).

Charles Ghigna's (1995) riddle poems, reminding Thomas of guessing games, were favorites. He considered the writing of cinquains, with their mathematical precision in syllable count for each of the five lines, like solving a math problem.

By way of an author study, we went online to gather information about Jack Prelutsky; I put together a selection of this author's books. Like dozens of other children, Thomas fell head over heels for Jack Prelutsky's sense of humor. He learned about onomatopoeia as he grew to love this poet's use of sound: the "chitter-chatter, chitter-chatter" of the chipmunk and the "hip-hop hoppity" of the rabbit in *Zoo Doings* (Prelutsky, 1983b, pp. 15, 28). He appreciated the marvelous made-up creatures (the snopp, for instance) that run through this poet's work.

Scholastic's website featured Jack Prelutsky, with his entertaining reading of a poem and his tips for young writers: "Keep a notebook for jotting down ideas. Poems take time to write and need to be revised again and again to get the right effect. Worry more about ideas and careful descriptions than about rhyme."

Prelutsky offered a first stanza for a poem, inviting children to finish it (and submit it for publication on the website, an exciting prospect).

When I awoke one morning,
A stork was on my head.
I asked, What are you doing there?
It looked at me and said . . .

The poet asked children to consider how different the poem would be if "stork" was replaced with "mouse," "moose," or "hawk." Thomas chose "hawk" for the bird on his head. Here is his second stanza:

I'm looking for some birdseed,
Small, crunchy, beige, and red,
But all I've found is the hair
That's sticking up on your head.

At the end of the project, Thomas listed some of the things he had learned about poetry. He now knew that some poems rhyme; others don't. Some are nonsense; some tell stories. Poems can be written in shapes. In lots of poems, things are compared to other things. Sound is important in poems; sounds can be like the things being talked about. Made-up words are okay in poetry; sometimes they can even make it better. Reading poems out loud makes them fun; sometimes you have to read slow and sometimes fast. To write some poems, like cinquains, you have to follow set rules in the way you do in puzzles and games. Writing poetry takes time.

I was surprised by how much Thomas learned from just having poetry read to him. This learning evolved from the *reading*, not from structured lessons. When poetry challenged Thomas, he took the challenge, not giving up on a poem because some of the vocabulary was unfamiliar to him. He simply asked for help in clarifying the meaning of these new words. Poetry became part of his life in an easy, unstilted way. The routine of reading poetry is established, something we both look forward to each night. Even when the evening is hectic, there is always time for a short poem.

Thomas has his own anthology of personally selected poems. He has added poetry books to his personal library. On a recent car trip, he brought Shel Silverstein's (1996) *Falling Up* and read aloud to his grandmother. Sharing these poems allows us to escape, laugh, look at the world in a new way, and enjoy ourselves. What potential for the family! What potential for the classroom!

Erica Giller and Niece and Nephew, Leora and Seth Bookman

A survey confirmed my suspicion that my niece, Leora, 13, and my 11-year-old nephew, Seth, had only desultory experience with poetry, in school or out. They seemed not to consider poetry of any importance in their literary lives. I set three goals for my project with them: to expose them to a range of poems and poetry; to show them that poems can take many forms,

> "When something is too beautiful or too terrible or even too funny for words: then it is time for poetry" (Eve Merriam, 1964, p. 1).

rhymed and unrhymed; and to convince them that poetry is enjoyable and worthwhile.

I first made an astonishing discovery: These children had never heard of Shel Silverstein and Jack Prelutsky, poets that are household names to most children of all ages. Having heard in the poetry class that humorous poetry is enjoyed most by a majority of children, I read aloud to Seth and Leora from Shel Silverstein, Jack Prelutsky, Judith Viorst, John Ciardi, Douglas Florian, and Jane Yolen. I asked which of the many poems they would recommend to a friend. Although Seth and Leora frequent the library for school assignments, they had never browsed in the poetry section, as I asked them to do. "I can't believe there are so many poems in the world," said Seth. Both children searched for books by Prelutsky and Silverstein.

As we read the poems, we noted how they were put together. They recognized that in Shel Silverstein's (1974) "Sick," "every two lines rhyme." This was an opportunity to introduce them to the term for this pattern: rhyming couplets. I asked them if they could add a couplet of their own to the poem. Leora obliged:

I hurt my leg and my knees,
I think my head has fleas.

Seth wrote:

My nose and eyes are red;
I think I should stay in bed.

The next step in recognizing form was to note how many poems contained quatrains, or two sets of rhyming couplets in a stanza. Inspired by Viorst's (1984) "Mother Doesn't Want a Dog" (p. 44), Seth wrote a quatrain:

My mother doesn't want a bird.
She says they'd make too much noise.
They'd fly around the house at night,
And mess up all our toys.

John Ciardi's "Mummy Slept Late While Daddy Fixed Breakfast" (in Cullinan, 1996, p. 40) inspired Leora to write:

My mother makes cookies;
They are hard as a rock.
Once I bit into one,
It tasted like sock.

We continued to read together, with an emphasis on humorous poems and those dealing with the children's special interests, like sports. As we read, the children noted that some poems did not rhyme. "Even though poems don't actually rhyme like a song," said Leora, "they do follow a rhythm."

Seth commented on "Foul Shot" by Edwin A. Hoey (1962): "The poem doesn't follow any pattern that I can see, no couplets, for instance, but the single words on a line add speed, make me feel as if I'm watching the game. You can't really get that with regular sentences."

This is an excerpt from "Foul Shot":

The ball
Slides up and out,
Lands,
Leans,
Wobbles.

In the poetry class, one of our assignments was to create a list poem using the contents of our handbags. I asked the children to get out their knapsacks and do the same. As we did in the poetry class, the children and I talked first about using poetic devices like comparisons and varied line lengths, as well as use of specific detail to make the list interesting.

Here is an excerpt from Seth's poem:

In my old friend,
the ripped briefcase,
I have a spelling book,
which I hate,
two pencils, and a pen,
a crumpled paper
with a hokey homework assignment from last week,
crumbs from a bag of cookies,
and three dimes and a nickel from snack money.

Leora's poem included this excerpt:

> Here's an interesting inventory:
> A ruler that I don't really use,
> Spare change,
> three quarters, two dimes, and seven pennies
> that jingle when I walk.
> My loose-leaf, decorated with decals,
> stickers of Disney and Looney Tunes characters.

My time with Leora and Seth was limited, so we were unable to work with cinquains, acrostics, and haiku, as I would have wished. Shape poems were a special interest of theirs from browsing in poetry books. In the end, I didn't need a survey to see how much they had learned and how their who-cares-about-poetry attitude had changed for the better.

Taking Georgia Heard's advice for our final work together, I invited them each to write a poem on a topic and in a form of their own choosing. In Chapter 2 of *For the Good of the Earth and the Sun* (1989) Heard says that the teacher must create with children an interest in and enjoyment of poems. I believe I did that and it worked. Both Leora and Seth chose to write with rhyme for their last poem of our study.

Homework by Seth Bookman

> Everyday at the end of school
> My teacher gives homework, not very cool.
> She makes us do math and spelling at home;
> I'd rather play or talk on the phone.
> I hate when we have to do writing work.
> Sometimes I think my teacher's a jerk.

My Favorite Little Brother by Leora Bookman

> I have a little brother named Elliott.
> Sometimes he is a pain.
> Once he took my favorite sticker
> And flushed it down the drain.

> He sucks his thumb and cries at night,
> He even pulls my hair;
> He messes up my room sometimes,
> And sits on my favorite chair.

Elliott follows me around the house;
I wish he'd follow another.
Sometimes I wonder why I still
Call him my favorite brother.

Christine Mehler and Friend Elizabeth

I babysit for my neighbor's daughter, Elizabeth (Liz), aged 10. She agreed to help me with the assignment for the poetry class, although she crinkled her nose in distaste when she found that the subject was poetry. When we began the project, to determine what she knew about poetry and her attitude toward it, I asked her a number of survey questions, including: "What comes to your mind when you hear the word 'poetry'?" Liz wrote, "It is hard work to read and write it." "Do you ever read poetry on your own?" I asked. "Not really," she said. Asked, "What do you like best about poetry?" she responded: "Nothing." I knew that I had to work hard to change Liz's knowledge of and attitude toward poetry.

Noticing from the survey that Liz liked poems that rhyme, I chose these for our first session, bringing, so as not to overwhelm her, only one book, *There's an Awful Lot of Weirdos in Our Neighborhood* (McNaughton, 1987). Together we looked through it and I read aloud some poems that she obviously enjoyed. I had her hooked and I didn't want to lose her.

Shape poems like those found in *Seeing Things* (Froman, 1974), *A Poke in the Eye* (Janeczko, 2001), and *Doodle Dandies* (Lewis, 1998a) came next. I wanted Liz to see that poems came in a variety of formats. She was intrigued, never having seen poems like these. She wrote one of her own:

Leaves
   f
   a
   l
   l
from the trees
in autumn.
I love the
   f
   a
   l

> "When I teach classes, I ask students to use the mask, to pretend to be something else. Some like to think of themselves as whirlwinds, tornadoes, or strong mountains. Others choose to pretend they are beautiful flowers" (Myra Cohn Livingston, 1991, p. 23).

l
i
n
g
leaves in all their colors.
They make a $_r$a^{inb}o$_w$
On the ground.

We tried acrostics, with Liz volunteering to write one using her name, following that with acrostics using my name, her brother's name, and her parents' names. I was encouraged by her creativity and especially her interest in what we were doing with poetry and verse. Here is the acrostic using her name:

Elizabeth is a
Likeable person who is very
Intelligent. She is a
Zoo lover, a lover of animals
And sports. She is a
Bright student who is
Excellent at
Table tennis, but she
Hates broccoli.

We dipped into several anthologies, reading a wide variety of poems. She found many reflected her own experiences; one about an allergy to cats she said "must have been written just for me!" Liz was surprised by the length of story poems; she'd always thought of poems as short. When she noted that many story poems were made up of four-line verses, I introduced her to *quatrain*, the term for these stanzas. She became adept at identifying quatrains, eagerly trying one of her own on the subject of an upcoming math test that made her anxious.

I have a math test in one day;
I don't want to go to school.
I wish that test would go away;
Math makes me feel a fool.

Liz and I spent happy hours reading poems to each other. She *was* hooked. We read poems she selected from books she checked out of the library. We wrote together. Liz started a personal anthology.

We staged a "poetry night" at Liz's house; her parents and grandparents listened as she read her own poems and favorites from her anthology.

We did an author study on Robert Frost. As a member of the chorus in elementary school, I had sung a choral version of Frost's (1979) "A Road Not Taken" (p. 105). I taught the melody to Liz, who loves to sing. She especially enjoyed hearing and reading Frost's poems about birds and animals, like "The Last Word of a Bluebird" (p. 135).

This project was an amazing experience for me. I feel I have really made a difference in Liz's life, opening her eyes to a whole new world. Poetry, which she once called "boring" and "hard work," is now exciting fun for her. I think the key was not to push poetry on her. I never forced her to do any reading or writing. I never questioned her about a poem's meaning or made her memorize poetic terms. I let her explore and discover on her own, subtly guiding her to new experiences. I think Liz always liked poetry; she just needed to give it a chance. I am proud of the survey she completed at the end of our time together.

After we had enjoyed poetry together, she gave new answers to the survey questions. Asked, "What comes to your mind when you hear the word 'poetry'?" Liz at first had complained that it was hard work to read and write it. The second time around, Liz wrote, "Poetry is fun and easy to read and write. I can write poems about anything I want. Poetry is something you can read and write to make you feel good." The old answer to the second question, "Do you ever read poems on your own?" was No; the new answer: "I read poetry on my own a lot now. I like shape and story poems the best." In the beginning Liz had said that she liked nothing about poetry. After our last session, this was her response: "What do I like best about poetry? It lets your thoughts explode on the page."

WORDS OF TEACHERS

Space doesn't permit further full accounts of the experiences of teachers in the poetry class. What follows in conclusion are their words of wisdom in brief, selected snippets from accounts of concerted efforts to bring children and poetry together to develop literacy. (For move sound advice on teaching poetry, consult the heroine of Sharon Creech's 2001 novel-in-verse, *Miss Stretchberry*.)

Pat Munsch

My fifth-grade children had little exposure to poetry when we began our study. I set out to give them experience reading, writing, listening to, and talking about poetry. To start, I brought in a variety of collections of poems, from Silverstein and Prelutsky to more classical writers like Robert Frost and Robert Louis Stevenson. I also included humorous poetry by David Harrison, David McCord, and Dennis Lee. Each day students in small groups picked a different book, reading, sharing, and discussing poems they liked, and finally sharing with the whole class. From our study, the children began to see what poets did to make their poems pleasing to the eye and ear. I drew a large toolbox and inside put the names of the poets' tools as we identified them: alliteration, rhyme, repetition, comparisons, and so on.

We tried to use these tools ourselves. In groups the children wrote about a small toy horse, some colorful shoelaces, and a blank piece of paper. The horse was a lonely stallion, missing his rider; the shoelaces were licorice string candy; the blank paper was a blanket of snow, waiting for our footprints, a cloud ready to burst with words.

The children chose their favorite poems for their poetry folders, covering the pages of anthologies with Post-it® notes. Many new poets were discovered, their names decorating the covers of the folders. Inside, favorite poems were carefully copied.

A new student, not reading at the same level as the others or as well-adjusted socially, had arrived in my class. He read Silverstein for many days, copying his favorites. When I introduced him to Walter Myers's book-length poem, *Harlem* (1997), he was captivated. He couldn't copy the entire book for his poetry folder, but he could and did copy favorite parts. He loved the book so much his mother bought it for him. Proudly, he showed it to me, declaring that now he could read it forever.

Michelle Cumming

Whenever I mentioned writing poetry to my fifth grade, I heard groaning, so I knew I had to be careful. We started with tongue twisters, which I didn't introduce as poetry, but as an exercise in playing with words. Of course, that is what much of poetry is: wordplay. Without knowing it, the students were working with a poetic device, alliteration, and enjoying themselves.

Marie Kontaroudis

I feel poems are very important to promote literacy in children. As we worked with poetry, it became a major part of our life in the classroom. Students enjoyed poems because they are usually short, easy, and fun to read. They are about life and feelings; they put common experiences insightfully into words. The children found that they could never get tired of poetry. There was something for everyone in the collections. Most poems could be read more than once and each time enjoyed for different reasons.

Carolyn Horvath

In just a few months, my entire third-grade class embraced poetry. They want to read it, listen to it, buy it through our book club orders, and write it every chance they get. Even Javier, who swore he hated poetry and always would, found three poems that make him laugh as he reads them again and again. Most of all, the children love poetry that rhymes and is humorous. But they can learn to love all types and forms of poetry. Everything is in the presentation: Let the poetry speak for itself.

Kathryn Kraemer

During the course of our study, my first-grade students were immersed in poetry. They experienced a variety of forms. They made many literacy connections, writing their own nonsense poems and tongue twisters. Listening skills were developed during our daily reading. In response to my oral reading of poems, the children tapped and nodded; one child said, "My head moved when your voice did."

To understand the poems fully, students had to listen for certain words and sounds, as well as pauses and phrasing. Writing skills grew out of individual and group activities. The use of poetry response journals encouraged reading and writing. Each time we read a poem that everyone enjoyed, I xeroxed it and the children added it to their journals. I found they voluntarily memorized favorite poems.

Eileen Finlay

To become teacher of poetry, I must be a reader of poetry. Reading through the booklists for the college class gave me the opportunity to discover new poetry and build my knowledge and interest in it. Having read myself and done some poetry writing, I feel more confident in teaching poetry and converting unsatisfied students into productive imaginers.

Jeorgia Stabile

I read the class the poem "My New York" in Chapter 3 of this book. I thought if these first graders heard a poem by children like themselves, it would spark interest in the genre. It worked. Most, perhaps all, of the poetry they ever read was written by adults. To hear the work of other children was a happy revelation.

Michele Carbone

In surveying my fifth-grade class, I think an important question was, "What do you want to learn or know about poetry?" Answers to this question helped me to respond to the needs and interests of my children. These were varied: How do you read poetry to get the sense? Where do poets get their ideas? Who are some good poets? What are some good poems? How hard is it to write a poem? How do you write a poem? Why do some poems rhyme and others don't?

Maria Sabella

At first it was hard for my fourth graders to appreciate poems by Langston Hughes because many lacked the rhyme the children were accustomed to. We began to discuss other ways poets use words. We talked about how they use words to describe and to compare to make you see things in new ways. We examined the language in Langston Hughes's (1995) "Dreams" (p. 32). Right away the children grasped the idea of figurative speech, understanding exactly what the poet meant when he compared life without dreams to a bird's broken wing and "a barren field frozen with snow."

Claudine Kroeger

I began to immerse my second graders in poetry from the first day of school, using poems about going back to school and making new friends. I read poems every spare minute: before lunch and as we got ready to leave for home. There was no formal teaching at this stage, just listening to and enjoying good poems. I hung poems on charts around the room. I began to notice children reading these poems in groups or on their own during snack and center time. They asked to copy them into their notebooks. They were making their own connections to poems. This was not something I could teach.

WORDS OF CHILDREN

Asked what poetry is, a second grader in Angela Pagnozzi's class replied, "Poetry rhymes. Well, not all the time. It has to make sense. It's like music without rhythm. No. It has rhythm. It's music without the band."

Cyndi Goldberg worked on a poetry project with her son, Ari, a sixth grader. "Do you think poetry can empower you," she asked. His answer: "Definitely. I can write about my feelings and I can write poems just for myself. I don't have to show them to anybody. Now I know it's okay to write a poem instead of a long essay when you have something to say. I learned that sometimes poetry can say more than prose can."

Alicia, in Catherine O'Sullivan's fifth grade, wrote couplets about her brother.

Andrew
My baby brother is new to me;
I was thrilled that he was a he.
He cries and cries in the late night;
Sometimes he gives us quite a fright.
I love to give him a great big hug,
Then just lie with him on the rug.

Admitting that he sometimes found poetry difficult to understand, Muaz, a third grader in Carolyn Horvath's class, explained, "Sometimes it feels mysterious because the poem at first doesn't make sense. Then, when I take another good look, it starts becoming sensible to me."

The Last Word

School
Has children
Filled with dreams
To share with others
Everyday.

—Kelly Maby, fifth-grade student
Teacher: Catherine O'Sullivan

References

Adoff, A. (1968). *I am the darker brother*. New York: Macmillan.

Adoff, A. (1973). *Black is brown is tan*. New York: Harper & Row.

Adoff, A. (1982). *All the colors of the race*. New York: Lothrop.

Adoff, A. (1994). *My black me: A beginning book of black poetry*. New York: Dutton. (Original work published 1974)

Angelou, M. (1993). *Life doesn't frighten me*. New York: Stewart, Tabori, & Chang. (Original work published 1978)

Aylesworth, J. (1998). *Old black fly* (S. Gammell, Illus). New York: Holt.

Ayre, J. (1989). *Northrop Frye: A biography*. New York: Random House.

Bayer, J. (1992). *A, My name is Alice*. New York: Dutton. (Original work published 1984)

Begay, S. (1995). *Navajo: Visions and voices across the mesa*. New York: Scholastic.

Brown, M. W. (2000). *I like bugs*. New York: Golden Books.

Bruchac, J. (1995). *The earth under sky bear's feet: Native American poems of the land*. New York: Philomel.

Bruchac, J. (1996a). *Between earth and sky*. New York: Harcourt.

Bruchac, J. (1996b). *Four ancestors: Stories, songs, and poems from native North America*. Mahwah, NJ: BridgeWater Books.

Chatton, B. (1993). *Using poetry across the curriculum*. Phoenix, AZ: Oryx Press.

Chigna, C. (1995). Riddle rhymes. New York: Hyperion.

Children's Book Council. (1997). Myra Cohn Livingston. In *Books remembered: Nurturing the budding writer* (pp. 31–35). New York: Children's Book Council.

Chukofsky, K. (1968). *From two to five*. Berkeley: University of California Press.

Cole, W. (1981). *Poem stew*. New York: Harper.

Copeland, J. (1993/1994). *Speaking of poets, Volumes I and II*. Champaign, IL: National Council of Teachers of English.

Creech, S. (2001). *Miss Stretchberry*. New York: HarperCollins.

Cullinan, B. (Ed.). (1996). *A jar of tiny stars*. Honesdale, PA: Boyds Mills.

Cullinan, B., Scala, M., & Schroder, V. (1995). *Three voices: An invitation to poetry across the curriculum*. York, ME: Stenhouse.

de Regniers, B. (1988). *Sing a song of popcorn: Every child's book of poems*. New York: Scholastic.

Dotlich, R. (2001). *Lemonade sun and other summer poems*. Honesdale, PA: Boyds Mills

Dunning, S., Lueders, E., & Smith, H. (Compilers). (1967). *Reflections on a gift of watermelon pickle*. Chicago: Scott, Foresman.

Esbensen, B. (1986). *Words with wrinkled knees*. New York: Crowell.

Fleischman, P. (1984). *I am phoenix*. New York: Harper.

Fleischman, P. (1985). *Joyful noise*. New York: Harper.

Florian, D. (1994a). *Beast feast*. New York: Harcourt.

Florian, D. (1994b). *Bing, bang, boing*. New York: Harcourt.

Florian, D. (1997). *In the swim*. New York: Harcourt.

Froman, R. (1974). *Seeing things: A book of poems*. New York: Crowell.

Frost, R. (1979). *Poetry of Robert Frost: The collected poems*. New York: Henry Holt.

Frye, N. (1963a). *The educated imagination*. Toronto: Canadian Broadcasting Corporation.

Frye, N. (1963b). *The well-tempered critic*. Bloomington: Indiana University Press.

Frye, N. (1970). *The stubborn structure*. Ithaca, NY: Cornell University Press.

Ghigna, C. (1995). *Riddle rhymes*. New York: Hyperion.

Glenn, M. (1996). *Who killed Mr. Chippendale?* New York: Lodestar.

Gollub, M. (1998). *Cool melons—Turn to frogs! The life and times of Issa*. New York: Lee & Low.

Harley, A. (2000). *Fly with me: An ABC of poetry*. Honesdale, PA: Boyds Mills.

Jarrell, R. (1964). The bat-poet (Illustrated by M. Sendak). New York: HarperCollins.

Harley, A. (2001). *Leap into poetry: More ABCs of poetry*. Honesdale, PA: Boyds Mills.

Heard, G. (1989). *For the good of the earth and the sun*. Portsmouth, NH: Heinemann.

Heard, G. (1999). *Awakening the heart*. Portsmouth, NH: Heinemann.

Hesse, K. (1998). *Out of the dust*. New York: Scholastic.

Hesse, K. (2001). *Witness*. New York: Scholastic.

Hoberman, M. A. (1991). *Fathers, mothers, sisters, brothers: A collection of family poems*. New York: Puffin.

Hoey, E. A. (1962). Foul shot. *Read*, 35(a), 29.

Hughes, L. (1995). *The collected poems of Langston Hughes*. New York: Vintage Books.

Jackson, H. (1951). *The complete nonsense of Edward Lear*. Mineola, NY: Dover.

Janeczko, P. (2000). *Teaching ten fabulous forms of poetry*. New York: Scholastic.

Janeczko, P. (2001). *A poke in the I*. Cambridge, MA: Candlewick.

Kennedy, X. J., & Kennedy, D. (1999). *Knock at a star*. Boston: Little, Brown.

Koch, K. (1970). *Wishes, lies, and dreams*. New York: Random House.

Koch, K. (1998). *Making your own days: The pleasures of reading and writing poetry*. New York: Scribner.

Kuskin, K. (1980). *Poetry explained* (Slides and audiotape). Weston Woods, CT: Weston Woods.

Lattimore, R. (1951). *The Iliad of Homer* (R. Lattimore, Trans. Chicago: University of Chicago Press.

Lear, E. (1991). *The nonsense poems of Edward Lear*. New York: Clarion.

Lee, D. (1977). *Garbage delight*. Toronto: Macmillan of Canada.

Lewis, J. P. (1996). *Riddle-icious*. New York: Knopf.

Lewis, J. P. (1998a). *Doodle dandies*. New York: Scholastic.

Lewis, J. P. (1998b). *Riddle-lightful*. New York: Knopf.

Livingston, M. C. (1991). *Poem-making: Ways to begin writing poetry*. New York: HarperCollins.

McClure, A., Harrison, P., & Reed, S. (1990). *Sunrises and songs*. Portsmouth, NH: Heinemann.

McCord, D. (1962). *Take sky*. Boston: Little, Brown.

McCord, D. (1970). *For me to say*. Boston: Little, Brown.

McMillan, B. (1990). *One sun: A book of terse verse*. New York: Holiday House.

McNaughton, C. (1987). *There's an awful lot of weirdos in our neighborhood*. Boston: Candlewick.

Martin, B., Jr. (1970). *Sounds I remember*. New York: Holt.

Merriam, E. (1962). *What can a poem do?* New York: Atheneum.

Merriam, E. (1964). *Inside a rhyme*. New York: Atheneum.

Merriam, E. (1973). *Out loud*. New York: Atheneum.

Myers, W. D. (1997). *Harlem* (C. Myers, Illus.). New York: Scholastic.

Milne, A. A. (1924). *When we were very young*. New York: Dutton.

Moore, C. C. (1999). *'Twas the night before Christmas*. (M. Craner, Illus.). New York: Harcourt.

Mora, P. (2000). *My own true name*. Houston: Piñata Books.

Most, B. (1999). *Four and twenty dinosaurs*. New York: Harper & Row.

Nash, O. (1980). *Custard and company: Poems by Ogden Nash* (Q. Blake, Illus.). Boston: Little, Brown.

Noyes, A. (1991). *The highwayman* (C. Keeping, Illus.). New York: Oxford University Press.

Oliver, M. (1994). *A poetry handbook: A prose guide to understanding and writing poetry*. New York: Harcourt.

Oliver, M. (1998). *Rules of the dance: A handbook for writing and reading metrical verse*. New York: Houghton Mifflin.

Opie, P., & Opie, I. (1955). *The Oxford nursery rhyme book*. New York: Oxford University Press.

Opie, P., & Opie, I. (1959). *The lore and language of schoolchildren*. New York: Oxford University Press.

Opie, P., & Opie I. (1992). *I saw Esau: The school child's pocket book*. Boston: Candlewick.

Padgett, R. (2000). *Handbook of poetic forms* (2nd Ed.). New York: Teachers and Writers Collaborative.

Prelutsky, J. (1983a). *The Random House book of poetry*. New York: Random House.

Prelutsky, J. (1983b). *Zoo doings*. New York: Greenwillow.

Prelutsky, J. (1984). *New kid on the block*. New York: Greenwillow.

Prelutsky, J. (1990). *Something big has been here*. New York: Greenwillow.

Prelutsky, J. (1996). *A pizza the size of the sun*. New York: Greenwillow.

Rasmussen, D., & Goldberg, L. (1976.) *A pig can jig* (Basic Reading Series, Level A, Part 2). New York: Science Research Associates.

Rosen, M. (1996). *Food fight: Poets join the fight against hunger with poems to favorite foods*. New York: Harcourt.

Schertle, A. (1995). *Advice for a frog*. New York: Lothrop, Lee & Shepard.

Silverstein, S. (1974). *Where the sidewalk ends*. New York: HarperCollins.

Silverstein, S. (1981). *A light in the attic*. New York: HarperCollins.

Silverstein, S. (1996). *Falling up*. New York: HarperCollins.

Sloan, G. (1981). Eve Merriam: A profile. *Language Arts, 58*(8), 957–964.

Sloan, G. (1991). *The child as critic: Teaching literature in elementary and middle school* (3rd ed). New York: Teachers College Press.

Sloan, G. (2001). But is it poetry? *Children's Literature in Education, 32*(1), 45–56.

Spivak, D. (1997). *Grass sandals: The travels of Basho.* New York: Atheneum.

Steinbeck, J. (1976). *The acts of King Arthur and his noble knights.* New York: Farrar, Straus & Giroux.

Tang, G. (2001). *The grapes of math: Mind stretching math riddles.* New York: Scholastic.

Terry, A. (1974). *Children's poetry preferences.* Champaign, IL: National Council of Teacher of English.

Tomlinson, C., & Lynch-Brown, C. (1993). *Essentials of children's literature: A critical handbook of children's literature.* New York: Allyn & Bacon.

Van den Huevel, C. (2000). *The haiku anthology* (3rd ed.). New York: Norton.

Viorst, J. (1984). *If I were in charge of the world.* New York: Atheneum.

Willard, N. (Ed.). (1998). *Step lightly: Poems for the journey.* New York: Harcourt Brace.

Wolfe, V. E. (2001). *True believer.* New York: Atheneum.

Yashima, T. (1977). *Umbrella.* New York: Puffin.

Index

About the Author

Glenna Sloan, a graduate of Teachers College, Columbia University, is a specialist in reading, language arts and children's literature. A teacher for 16 years in elementary and middle school, she now teaches graduate courses in children's literature in the School of Education at Queens College of the City University of New York. Her publications include *The Child as Critic: Teaching Literature in Elementary and Middle School*, numerous articles on teaching literature, and three novels for young people. An active member of the Children's Literature Assembly of the National Council of Teachers of English (NCTE), she also serves on the NCTE Poetry Award committee and is past president of the International Reading Association's (IRA) Special Interest Group for Reading and Children's Literature. She edits the children's book column of *Bookbird*, official publication of the International Board on Books for Young People. In 2001, Dr. Sloan received the IRA's Arbuthnot Award for Outstanding Teacher of Children's and Young Adult Literature.